THE CLOSET SPIRITUALIST

Waking up to one's "Truth" is the hardest thing you will ever do!

lulu

FRANCO A. ROMERO

For more information, visit us at: www.theclosetspiritualist.com

Questions or comments can be sent to: info@theclosetspiritualist.com

ISBN: 978-1-716-42773-2
eBook ISBN: 978-1-716-39456-0

Printed in the United States of America

Library of Congress Cataloging-in-Publication Data is available upon request.

Edited by Sharlene Romero

Book design and illustrations by
Diane Napper, Taurus Moon Graphic Design, LLC

Author photo by Savannah Romero

(First Edition)

Lulu Press, Inc., 627 Davis Dr., #300, Morrisville, NC 27560
www.lulu.com

Dedication

To humanity,

Know that you are so much more than you have been taught to believe. That within you lies the light that creates worlds. A Truth that will soon shine brightly for all to see.

and have been there for me in ways you will never know. I am proud to be your father and am blessed to call each of you my best friend. I love you all to God and back!

To my mother Alicia and father Jose Francisco, though you passed long ago into the world of infinite possibilities, I feel your presence each and every day. There isn't a week that goes by that I am not reminded of you and the heroism of your life. So many lessons learned from the paths you chose to take. Lessons that would serve as time capsules for me to discover later in life. Though you both led very distinct lives relative to your faith, know that you had a profound impact on the insights I would have in my quest for the Truth. I love you so much and can't wait to see you again in my dreams.

To my big brothers Jairo and Nestor Paul and my big sister Luz Elena, the three of you hold a special place in my heart. Not only are you the greatest siblings a kid could ever ask for, but I consider you to be among some of the most loving people in my life. Though I have not always been there for you, know that my love for you is undeniable. You are and always will be among the greatest heroes in my life.

To my loving friends, I cannot tell you how much you mean to me. There was a time in my life when I wondered if I would be blessed to have the friends I have now. I can honestly say, that with you in my life, I am the richest man alive when it comes to friendships. In my eyes, you are like family to me. I have and will continue to cherish our time together. I am honored to be your friend and look forward to having you in my life forever.

Lastly, I want to acknowledge my astral family. For years, I knew you only in my visions and dreams. Angelic beings whose images have een engrained in my mind since I can remember. Oh, how much I ve missed you. I know that with each passing day, the veil that has separated our two worlds is fading away and that someday soon we will be together again. Until then, I take solace in knowing that you are with me in spirit and will always be there to guide me with your light.

Contents

Foreword

It is not by accident that this book has found its way into your life; nor, that you are reading these words at this precise moment. You were meant to be here to read, process, and live out the prescient words inscribed onto these pages by my good friend, Franco Romero. I say this not from any place of authority but from personal experience, for this book appeared in my life at the precise moment I needed it most.

Though Franco and I have been friends for over 30 years, for the past two decades he and I have experienced the kind of soft estrangement close friends sometimes experience. Life happened – children, careers and the clanging discord of modern life caused us to drift in different directions. Synchronicity, however, would conspire to bring us back together again.

My father and Franco's mother-in-law, Joyce Arbuckle, died on the same week in January of 2019. That death would bring Franco [illegible] me together is important to understand because if you are to [illegible] from this book (and believe me, you will), you will need t[illegible] old self die so that the new you, the true and authentic [illegible] instinctively know lies within, can be reborn.

I came to learn of Joyce's death when I went to see if my father's obituary had been published in the Sunday newspaper. Unbeknownst to Franco, I decided to attend her funeral and following a brief reunion, we agreed to reconnect over coffee. That one coffee led to a series of other coffees (actually, chai teas) over the spring and summer months that would follow.

It didn't take long to see that Franco was "coming out" of his spiritual closet while I was still stumbling around, searching for the light switch in the darkness of my own spiritual reality. By the fall, Franco began to share drafts of his manuscript and although the intent was simply to ask for my feedback as a friend and author, I found myself benefitting immensely from the wisdom that laid within the pages of his book.

It has been said that mystics are not gifted people, but rather each person is a gifted kind of mystic. Franco is indeed a gifted mystic. But understand that you too are gifted. That you have a special role to play in the world to come. That without your unique voice, the chorus and its music that will trumpet the coming of this new world, will be incomplete.

Before diving into this gem of a book, my advice to you would be this – be not afraid. This book is meant to reveal what you already know but have forgotten. A longing for the truth that you deeply desire. All that is required is for you to penetrate the inner darkness and rediscover your eternal light. To that end, I encourage you to read this book with your heart, not your mind. If you do, I guarantee that the optical delusions that currently occupy your thoughts will give way to the unstruck melodies of your heart. You will soon find the silence to listen and heed to your heart's calling as it leads you back home to the world that awaits you.

Jack Uldrich
Author of *Higher Unlearning & Unlearning 101*
Minneapolis, Minnesota
January 2020

Introduction

There is something extraordinary happening to humanity right now. Something that is not visible to the naked eye, but yet its presence is being felt by millions all over the world. An Awakening that was promised to us long ago but whose purpose was distorted and ultimately forgotten over time. To fully embrace this Awakening will require you to let go of everything you were taught to believe. To break away from the social conditioning that has kept you hostage to your mind all these years. To let go of your dependency of the ego construct and the analytical mind which have controlled your pathological behaviors since birth.

Admittedly, what is being asked of you will be much easier said than done. Which is why I decided to tell my story now. To come out of the proverbial closet to share not only my spiritual quest, but to do so in the most vulnerable way possible. I knew I would have to go back into the murky waters of my tortured past. A past I vowe would never revisit, much less allow it to be chronicled for the world to see. It would take everything in me to go down again. But I knew deep down inside there was somethin needed to be said. As if someone was asking me to that had already been told in so many ways, by so many teachers, for thousands of years. Something that would be extremely important to humanity's quest for the Truth.

Within this story, I would have to disclose my most intimate secret of my clairvoyant abilities to channel a higher Consciousness. One that had been communicating with me since I was a little boy. A relationship that has grown into a beautiful friendship over the years. But that wasn't always the case. For years, I did everything I could to sabotage this relationship. To pretend it didn't exist. I was scared of who or what this voice represented. Back then, there was simply no place to turn to that wasn't likely to judge me as psychotic, delusional or spiritually possessed. So to avoid all the stigma, I locked my abilities away in the darkest regions of my mind.

Never in my wildest dreams did I expect to experience the transformation I went through as I wrote this book. Never could I have imagined that I would be surrendering myself to something infinitely greater. A voice that was calling me from deep within. Urging me to let go and remember the Truth regarding my higher Self and spiritual purpose. For this Truth would have tremendous consequences for the untold millions who have, or would soon be, experiencing their own Awakening.

In time, I came to realize that it wasn't just my story I needed to tell. That embedded within it were messages written in a language that only the heart could understand. Messages that were meant to assist humanity on its path to spiritual enlightenment. Messages that would allow each and every one of you to raise your level of consciousness so that frequencies all over the world could rise as well. A metaphysical process that would hold the key by which the light of this new Awakening would enter.

So you see, my story has as much to do with you as it does with me. It has to do with all of us and why we chose to come here at this particular moment in time. As such, there is so much I want to share with you. My collaboration with higher Consciousness has led to so many epiphanies. But if you approach this book with your analytical mind you will miss the messages you were meant to hear. You will come to repeat your past over and over again. Never realizing how close you came to finding the Truth about your higher Self. You will walk away frustrated that the only messages you received were those that were written in black and white. The majority of which you will discard as being trivial or commonsensical relative to your survival in this physical reality.

Do not be frustrated, for the answers you seek lie within. Not just within this book but within yourself. Answers that will reveal themselves if you promise to go into this having the faith of a child. To check your ego at the door and suspend your beliefs as much as you can. To close your eyes and allow yourself to imagine that maybe, just maybe, what you are about to hear is the Truth that you have been searching for all your life. Not my Truth, but rather a higher Truth from somewhere deep within the stillness that exists in all of us.

An understanding that you came here to do something great and the time to do so is now. That within you lies the power to literally create new worlds. To live a life full of peace, love, happiness and spiritual freedom. That by discovering your greatness, you will share your light with humanity as it goes through its own Awakening.

A transformation of consciousness so great that it will change th course of human history. So profound that it will require the colle energies of all to ensure that when it happens, it does so in the most magnificent and loving way imaginable!

Franco A. Romero
St. Louis Park, Minnesota
January 2020

Chapter One

Coming Out

It takes a considerable amount of bravery to come out to the world. The act of doing so is often very painful for the person that is doing the "coming out." Too often we see the unnecessary drama that unfolds when family, friends and acquaintances – not to mention society as a whole – publicly display their horror, disappointment, anger and disbelief at the news. As if somehow the person coming out was to blame for the insecurities of others.

What is never seen, however, is the internal struggle that one faces when coming out to themselves. We lose sight of the fact that years before someone comes out, a horrible war was waged within them to even get to this point. A denial on their part to accept their own individuality. An unwillingness to see themselves as different in a beautiful way rather than socially unacceptable to the world. It is this struggle that has led many to isolate themselves socially or worse yet, act out in hatred, anger, frustration and when all else would fail, commit suicide.

For years, I was guilty of being insensitive to the plight of these beautiful souls. I would turn a deaf ear to those coming out in matters pertaining to their true identity. Never giving it much thought as to the ordeal they must have gone through at the hands of others, not to mention their own worse critic, themselves. The irony of it all was that, I too, was experiencing the same ordeal, but somehow could not relate those struggles with what others were going through.

To those who have had the courage to come out and express themselves freely, I applaud and admire you. Your willingness to stand up and say, "This isn't right. I am who I am and I know that God loves me," is a testament of who you are as a loving, spiritual being in these times of turmoil. It is your uniqueness and your willingness to stand up for yourself that should be celebrated, not condemned. For it is this uniqueness that creates the genuine diversity of our beautiful planet. As such, we should protect it as we would any other fundamental right by which we exist as human beings.

It was this passion for the Truth that inspired me to come out to myself and proudly proclaim my spirituality. To say, "I refuse to deny who I am by hiding in shame. I refuse to live my life trapped in the closet of my seclusion. I will no longer fear being chastised by others for my beliefs. I will share the Truths as they have been shared with me by my spiritual teachers and the divinity in me I call God."

I share these Truths from the standpoint that they are as fundamental to you as they are to me. And thus, they speak to you as "Spirit" rather than the physical being you have known yourself to be. I know they may not resonate with your rational mind, but I promise they will find salvation in places deep within where you have all but forgotten. Whether you choose to do anything regarding these Truths is entirely up to you. To me, I can humbly say that they saved my life.

I want to start with the most fundamental Truth in all of creation – that is, there is only unconditional love. Love is the fabric by which the physical universe is held together. There is no other Truth that defines us more clearly as spiritual beings. It resides within the core of our spiritual essence which explains why we feel so empty when disconnected from it. Our desire to be defined by this Truth is what keeps us from falling asleep in a world that imposes a maddening set of belief systems that run contrary to our natural state of existence. It is the cornerstone of all Truths. And in my life, it has been the inspiration I have used to stay awake and realize that something has always been inherently wrong with this reality.

The second Truth holds that everything, be it seen or unseen, is made up of energy. That we live in a vibrational universe, not a physical reality. So why should you care? Because if everything is energy then everything is connected. And if everything is connected then there is no beginning and no end to that energy. So if everything is energy, then it stands to reason that God is energy. But not just any energy, a conscious energy that has no beginning and no end.

So if everything is connected, then "everyone" is connected, with no beginning and no end. Then I ask you, how is it possible that we can be so "disconnected" from a God, who by default, is part of the same energy? It makes absolutely no sense whatsoever, and yet the overwhelming majority of our world has accepted this notion of disconnection to be true. That somehow God is somewhere *out there*. To steal a line from one of my favorite movies – it's inconceivable!

The Truth is that we are all the same energy. Therefore, WE ARE ALL GOD! To be more exact, you and I are individual expressions of God experiencing duality in this physical reality. I know this is hard to comprehend, but I cannot stress the enormity of what is being said. Close your eyes and try to understand this extraordinary Truth, for it holds the key by which to open your door to your true identity.

Contrary to what you have been led to believe, you and God are One experiencing reality through this avatar you call your body. As such, you have the power to create your own reality. You came into this world knowing this Truth but have forgotten due to the onslaught of social conditioning that has been forced upon you by others. It is time now for you to wake up and reclaim your rulership of this Truth. For many of you this will not be easy, for you will fight this Truth every step of the way. I know because I did the same.

Know that your world is littered with clues left behind by you to help you remember. Yes, I did say "you," for you have been here before and I promise that before I finish this book, I will come back to this amazing point. For now, know that it is you who has chosen to stay oblivious to these Truths. "But why?" you will ask. "Why would I do that to myself?" Perhaps the timing wasn't right or maybe you came here to expose yourself slowly to these Truths. No matter the reason, you have reached a point in your evolution where these Truths can no longer stay hidden, and one way or another, they will come out.

> *As a child, I lived a rather nomadic life. Moving from one place to another for no apparent reason. Looking back, I often wondered if this was my parent's way of running from their past. A way to start fresh with a clean slate in life. I guess I'll never really know since my parents are both deceased now.*
>
> *There was one particular house that I will never forget. We moved into it when I was about five years old. It was the first house we had moved into. Up until then we had lived in apartments. Even back then I recall how excited I was to live in a house. To live*

among others in a neighborhood of homes. To have a backyard to play in and a garage for our car.

The euphoria I felt would not last long. Shortly after moving in my brother began behaving erratically. He was no more than nine or ten when he began to act out in fear. Over time, these episodes would become extremely intense. He no longer wanted to go to school and would spend his days in his room.

My parents, who had always had a rocky relationship, were constantly arguing. My father, who was an alcoholic, was struggling with his depression that was never diagnosed correctly. My mother did everything she could to keep our family from crumbling into the abyss; all while fighting her own personal demons of regret, resentment and worthlessness for the life she had inherited.

If that had been all, I would have said our life was rather typical of some families back then; sadly, even more so today. However, one night my brother woke up to an eerie feeling and a sound that was coming from the porch next to our kitchen. For whatever reason, he was drawn to its call and like a bad horror movie, he got up to investigate.

As he peeked out from our bedroom, he noticed the silhouette of a man standing in the dark. The man called to him with piercing red eyes. My brother panicked like anyone would and went screaming down the hall to my parents' bedroom. We all woke up to the sounds of his hysteria only to find out that there was nobody in the porch as he had claimed. Assuring him that it was all just a nightmare, we went back to sleep and thought nothing more of it.

That night would mark the beginning of five tumultuous and extremely bizarre years in my life. Years that would expose me to the supernatural. And though the chilling aspects of these events would consume me for years, I often look back with wonder at the clues they left behind. Clues that would foreshadow what was to come in my life. I can remember lying in bed many nights hearing strange noises from our attic. Since my bed was along the wall adjacent to the stairwell, I had become accustomed to hearing footsteps of what I sensed was an old man. As strange as it might sound, I could feel the weight of his tortured life as he carried himself up to the attic.

Throughout it all, there was always this voice. This beautiful, gentle voice assuring me that there was nothing to fear and that everything would be alright. "Do not be afraid," it would whisper in my ear. "It cannot hurt you, for your light shines brightly." Over time, the voice would explain why this spirit in our home was so unhappy. That despite the energies of fear present in our family, there was also a tremendous amount of love; thus, it was very resentful of that emotion. Resentful, since it once had that light but no longer knew how to get it back.

Though I could fill a book with the terrifying events that went on in that house for years, that was not my intent for telling you this story. For underneath it all, I remember having this calming presence in my

> *life. And though I would never see this presence with my own eyes, I often wondered if this was what was meant by having an imaginary friend.*
>
> *Regardless of the circumstances, I never thought of it as anything unusual. I just knew this voice to be a companion I could always count on. That is of course until a few years later when I stopped believing in such things as imaginary friends or guardian angels. In time, the voice would grow silent and the angel I once knew as my closest friend would disappear from my life.*

I am not here to sell anyone on mysticism nor to conjure up fears of the supernatural. Nor am I here to spread any conspiracy theories as to why we would deny ourselves of these Truths. I am merely stating that for whatever reason these Truths have been left out from our spiritual past. Leaving us to accept these ridiculous ideas about our relationship with God. Leaving us to put the pieces together in whatever manner life was willing to present us with. In my case, it began with a series of supernatural occurrences, but in yours it could have started differently.

Regardless of the circumstances, there is now hope and it lies within what is being discovered in our new sciences. Disciplines who stand by the basic premise that the universe is all connected by one energy source. But not just any energy source, an energy made up of consciousness. As I will discuss later in this book, this general acceptance has opened the door to a future reality unfathomable to the human mind in its current state of beingness.

For those that grasp these Truths, know that doubts and fears may overwhelm you, but these are perfectly normal. If anything, their contrast will push you even closer to your desires. Nevertheless, these

Truths will take a significant toll on your fragile ego. An ego that has been repeatedly thrown under the bus for being the culprit of your fears. As such, way before many of you will come out – and sadly way after – you will torture yourselves with guilt and shame.

You will allow yourselves to be viewed as crazy, delusional or strange; a social outcast, inferior to all including yourselves. And why? Because you have been led to believe that even God cannot love you the way you are. I ask you, does this make any sense? I mean, what unconditionally-loving God would act this way?

Before coming out to family and friends about my spirituality, I cannot tell you the agony I went through trying to reconcile this incredibly liberating state of beingness with the so-called "belief systems" society was forcing me to accept. Belief systems that I knew in my heart simply did not make sense. To me, the most difficult belief to reconcile was this issue of a disconnected and vindictive God.

As far back as I can remember, I simply could not reconcile this view with everything I knew to be true about my life. "If God made me in his image, why does the idea of a vindictive God feel so inherently wrong?" This question would torment me for years, but none more so than when I began my quest for the Truth. A quest that would ultimately lead to my complete surrender and subsequent awakening to the divinity that is me. A realization that the world we were led to believe is simply someone else's illusion. Or as I would argue – someone else's "delusion."

A third Truth holds that God speaks to us in so many different ways. Some more direct than others. You might hear God speaking to you as a voice in your head, heart or even gut which you often call your intuition. Sometimes it could just be in something you hear or maybe something you have read. Often times, it could be something you simply came across many years ago and are now recalling it from memory.

For instance, among the many childhood stories that left a memorable impression, none was more profound than the book *The Emperor's New Clothes.* Even as a child, I could not help being drawn to its obvious message. Yet, as empowering as this book was at the time, there was always this voice reminding me that later in life, I too, would fall victim to the plight of ignorance. So distorted would my mind become that it would require the attribute of love, among others, to recognize the Truth about my reality.

"And what was that?" you ask. That my mind had become the very prison I would fear in my physical reality. That I would willingly accept its sentence to live a life created entirely by the social construct rather than becoming the true creator of my own world. For those who are not acquainted with this beautiful book, allow me to summarize, for the moral of its story is so profound that I believe it is among the main reasons why you are here reading this book.

> *There was once an emperor who loved clothes almost as much as he loved himself. He had a different pair of clothing for each day of the year. Nothing but the finest would do. One day, two strangers appeared claiming they could weave the most magical pieces of clothing imaginable. So magical were they that only the wise ones could see them.*
>
> *The emperor was overwhelmed with vanity. He ordered the two weavers to make him magical clothing and paid them a king's ransom to do so. A week later, the men came back with clothing that could not be seen by the naked eye. They convinced the emperor*

> *that only the ignorant and weak among them could not see their splendor.*
>
> *Not wanting to seem foolish, the emperor convinced himself that as ridiculous as it appeared, their story had to be true. Worse yet, the emperor's subjects went along with the deception, fearing they too would be ridiculed for their stupidity. Before long, deception had become reality, and had it not been for the innocence of one child, things would have stayed that way.*
>
> *"You have no clothes," the child exclaimed as the emperor walked by one day. Immediately, everyone looked at each other and began to laugh. Embarrassed by the truth, the emperor blushed as he went on his way, pretending as if he still had clothes.*

In life, you are that child and these Truths I speak of are in each one of you. Truths that have been dormant all these years until now. Know that it is time to wake up and that the process of doing so should never feel terrifying to you for any reason. Know that you are not the only one waking up to these Truths. There are millions who are feeling what you are experiencing and many more will follow. A sense of surrealism that may make you question your sanity only to realize that it is not you that is insane.

The fourth Truth holds that we are undergoing a tremendous change in our world. But it is not the change you may be thinking of when someone brings this matter to light. It is both an external and internal change that is affecting the global consciousness of our planet. Since this will be discussed in greater detail later in the book, for now know that this change cannot happen without you. As Gandhi once said, "You must be the change you wish to see in the world."

I know many of you will struggle to internalize, much less embrace what I am telling you. Remember, your biggest critic is not that which you see externally, but that which you cannot see internally. How many times have you already questioned or criticized what you have read in these pages? How many of you have already felt guilt or even offense at the words that are being written? For those who believe in these words, how many times have you already questioned if this could be "too good to be true?" For what it's worth, I know what you are going through because I lived in this state of denial for most of my life.

As in Plato's *The Republic,* it is so easy to falsely accuse yourself of being crazy; thus, imprisoning yourself to a life of misery. Accepting the haunting figures on your walls as your true reality rather than to face the "calling" that has been relentless in drawing you back to the Truth – to YOUR Truth! A calling so great that ignoring it has become torture. It is no wonder that your higher Self, the God in you, has drawn you to this book right here, right now.

By "God" I mean whatever Supreme Being you align yourself with because God is God no matter what name you give it. This is yet another Truth you know but your rational mind cannot, or in some cases, will not accept. I tell you now that you are being drawn to this Truth because you know that labels do not define this thing we call God. All it does is create divisiveness. A duality that does not need to exist, yet it causes us to turn on each other in the name of whatever label you give this benevolent being. Have we stooped so low as to think that God was created in our image? That it would care about such trivial issues as to what label we give it? Again, how can this make sense to any rational being, much less a spiritual being such as God?

Know that this entire book is filled with many Truths. More Truths than you can imagine, and yet inherent in all of you. As such, they will be revealed to you in time as some are being revealed to you now. It is up to you to decide which, if any, call you. "But how will I know these Truths when they come?" you will ask. You will know them simply because they will run contrary to everything you have been exposed to in your social construct. More importantly, you will know them because they will bring forth a light that will make you feel alive again!

Throughout my life, I have found myself running into the same road blocks that most of you will encounter who are reading this book. These concepts were as foreign to me when I first heard them as they will seem to you. But as foreign as they will seem to you, there will be a voice or a sixth sense that will keep pulling you in as if somewhere or in some other place and time you've lived these Truths before.

Most of us will brush these feelings aside, downplaying their importance. "Oh, it's only my imagination," you will say. But as you will soon discover, your imagination is the gateway to your soul. It offers a glimpse of who you really are and where you came from. Hence, why it must be nurtured rather than discarded as foolish or worthless.

There is yet another Truth I am compelled to share with you now, if only briefly. It has to do with faith and its ability to make all our dreams come true. All my life, I thought I understood this concept we call faith. It certainly has been tossed around freely enough – but what is it? Faith is the intangible sense by which we believe in ourselves. It has nothing to do with believing in anything that makes up our outer reality.

For me, this particular Truth was extremely hard to accept because it forced me to realize that everything I desired in life – peace, love happiness, and spiritual freedom – was a function of how I viewed myself. That the outer world was simply a reflection of the inner reality in me. That my faith in me, the inner Truth that I was One with God, was the secret by which I could be the deliberate creator of not just my dreams, but of reality itself. This is not some philosophical concept I picked up along the way, but rather the keys to the kingdom of God which many of our greatest teachers and ancient traditions have alluded to.

This Truth should rock you to your core. It did for me. To be honest, it scared the hell out of me and I know it will scare many of you too. But here is where you need to trust yourself; to have faith and let this quest unfold. Stay open to what this book will share, for it is speaking to you as if it were telling your story. You see my story is no different than yours. Yes, we may have different backgrounds and our circumstances may not be the same, but at the end of the day – here you are seeking the same Truth.

This quest has as much to do with you as it does about me. We are reflections of each other. This too is yet another Truth. I know there will be times when you will hate what you hear in my words. You may even wind up being my worst critic, but that's fine with me. The beauty in all of this is that the human spirit, that which we refer to as our soul or life energy, knows only the Truth which is universal no matter how we choose to interpret it. In other words, your interpretation of Truth is as right to you as mine is to me.

Lastly, I want to share a few thoughts that may help you as you examine your life within the context of this book. First, I call my life experiences a "quest" rather than a journey and ask you to consider doing the same. Why? Because going on a quest allows me to view life as an adventure, full of intrigue and magic. While a journey feels too much like a struggle, as though I were looking for answers *out there* through someone else's reality.

My quest for the Truth required a tremendous amount of soul searching. That does not mean, however, that you are expected to do the same; at least, not in the manner in which I did it. In fact, it is my desire that this book will serve as a blueprint by which you will search out the answers to your own quest in whatever manner pleases you most. To find profound meaning relative to your own existence as a beautiful reflection of God.

To that end, I will do my best to share these Truths as they have been revealed to me in a way that will enhance your own spiritual and religious experience. In no way am I expressing a particular viewpoint relative to any religious belief system. That is not at all my intent. In fact, it matters little to me what your belief systems may be relative to your spirituality or religion. They are but different pathways to God. There is an ancient parable that sums this point up beautifully.

> *Several blind people were asked to touch a different part of an elephant. They were asked to describe what they were touching. To compare the elephant to something they knew. One blind man touched the leg of the elephant and described it like a tree. Another touched the tail and said it was like a rope. The one standing at the tusk said the elephant was like a spear. The one by the ear said the elephant was like a fan. Yet, the one standing by its side said the elephant was like a wall.*

The moral here is that we all have our own views of the Truth and that's fine. We need to go beyond what we believe is the "only" Truth to embrace the notion that the Truth has many faces by which to see its beauty. That our experiences are simply one possibility of the Truth; one unique perspective of it. That when we come to appreciate the beauty of our diversity, so will we come to awe and respect the multifaceted views we have of the same Truth.

I want you to know that this book is not meant to be a philosophical or scholarly dissertation on life designed to convince you that it should be your Truth. Nor is it my intention to impress you with academic, religious or scientific references. Therefore, I will refrain from making such references since I am not here to prove anything that you don't already know but have forgotten. As I have noted, the Truths I speak of have been known for thousands of years, but only now are they being revealed through the global awakening of our planet.

I encourage you to do your own research or go on your own quest, however you define that. The internet is a tremendous resource for knowledge and a superconductor for resonant energy. In other words, what you seek is seeking you. Therefore, if you are willing to be open and honest with yourself, finding your Truth will never be easier. How "easy" will depend on how far down the rabbit hole you want to go. It is my advice that you go as far as you can, for what lies beyond its darkness is an unimaginable light of pure consciousness that is ready to set you free.

I also encourage you to explore the practice of channeling. I define channeling as the ability by which to find a quiet, peaceful place – both in your heart and mind – that enables you to align with higher Consciousness for the purpose of enlightenment. Contrary to what we have come to believe, we all possess the ability to channel. It does not require one to reach a deep meditative state. In fact, many of you are channeling daily but may not even know it. For instance, when you are focused on something with great conviction or passion, you are channeling. When you are daydreaming, you are channeling. When you wake up in the morning and allow yourself to quietly entertain the inspiring thoughts that come to you from out of nowhere, you are channeling.

Channeling allows you to tune into an entirely different frequency of consciousness. You are literally tuned into a vibrational pattern that often involves a spontaneous collaboration between the digestive, heart and brain regions of your body. A phenomenon unknown to science until recently. You see this with artists, writers, motivational speakers, actors and musicians but it is not restricted to just them. It is through channeling that many of these Truths have been revealed to me in conversations I have had with higher Consciousness. Many more will be revealed if you stay open to using such practices of inner exploration. I cannot stress enough that nothing will change in life if you are unwilling to first change your inner reality – for your sake, not anyone else's.

Put differently, the universe is a reflection of your thoughts and emotions. If you view yourself negatively, then the world you see will manifest in a negative way. If you view yourself positively, then the world you will manifest will be your oyster. I will tell you now that this has been the hardest thing to do in my life, for I was never taught the magic of self-reflection and introspection. Yet, it was and still is the most liberating experience of my life. And, I assure you that if you are willing to answer your inner calling to seek out the Truth, you will never be the same again.

Finally, why now? Why have you been drawn to this book? Why are these words speaking to you? Why is there this sense that things don't seem the same anymore? That something deep within you is trying to come out and proclaim your greatness? Understand that nothing happens that isn't intended to happen in its perfect time. That you have chosen this moment based on everything you have done in your life to date. In other words, there is nothing that you should or should not have done up until now. No matter how painful or unpleasant they may have been, it was all perfectly orchestrated by you to get to this exact moment in your life. "And where exactly is that?" you will ask.

To be honest, a place that seems quite foreign to you, and yet you've been there before. Perhaps when you were young or more likely in a different life or maybe that place in between lives you call home. We feel it in a way that our minds cannot fully comprehend. There are moments where life simply does not make sense. You catch yourself taking a step back knowing that there is something more to this reality than what others have led you to believe.

Often times, it comes at the most heightened periods in your life where things seem to be reaching a climactic moment of pain or suffering. It is in these moments that you feel a tug from deep within reminding you of your true desires in life. And yes, we have been conditioned nicely to believe that "no pain is no gain" or that we were born into original sin, and therefore our struggles are meant to show God how faithful we are to him. We have come to believe that God wants us to toil in our misery either for our sins or because he is testing our free will to be obedient. Nothing could be further from the truth.

You are here to realize what many throughout time have come to understand, that this reality is about one thing and one thing only – to co-create a world based on every desire you have had for peace, love, happiness and spiritual freedom. You are here because we have reached a point in humanity's evolution whereby as spiritual beings, we have experienced every form of contrast imaginable.

It is time now for us to evolve into a new world whereby we become "deliberate" creators of our reality. To evolve into a higher form of frequency that exists right now on this planet but simply cannot be seen in our current state of vibrational existence. As we transition into this higher frequency, we will also be paving the way for a new class of spiritual beings to emerge. A class that will co-create and experience its own reality in the lower vibrations of this physical universe.

For those who are coming out of your "spiritual closet," know that you are doing so because you have chosen to be a light to this world. To be the first among you who are awakening to what "can be" rather than "what is." You are here because you know that what exists now is not your reality and just like the lucid dreams of your past, there is an internal clock or voice telling you to wake up and bear witness to these Truths.

Shakespeare once said, "All the world is a stage and all the men and women merely players." But players to whom? To you of course. For you are God experiencing itself, yourself, in this magnificent body. As such, you are the writer, producer, director and performer of your play. The play of life you came here to deliberately create with others for the sole purpose of ushering in the greatest evolution of human consciousness ever to exist on this planet!

Chapter Two

The Dream State

As a child, I had this uncanny ability to wake up from a nightmare by consciously experiencing myself as the observer rather than the participant in the dream. Whenever fear presented itself, I would immediately switch roles and become this voice deep within, reminding me that everything was simply an illusion. To wake up, I would focus on my intention, shake my head forcefully, and tell myself, "It's only a dream!" And just like that it would be over. The curious thing was that sometimes it wasn't over. I would lay in bed believing I was awake only to realize that I was reliving this horrifying experience in a new dream. Unwilling to accept the reality of what I thought were my five senses, I would repeat the process over and over again until I was finally awake.

I learned later in life that what I had experienced as a child is referred to as "lucid" dreaming – the ability to realize and deliberately manipulate your dreams. For years, I thought this was normal. That everyone had these dreams so I discarded their importance. But as I got older, I found myself going back to those dreams, seeking answers to their significance as if a clue or riddle was hidden within each one. I couldn't shake this feeling that somehow these dreams had something to do with my physical reality.

By the time I reached my late teens, I could sense that my interpretation of the world wasn't quite lining up with what I had been taught to believe. I was beginning to feel the presence of a voice that was different than the reasoning voice I had come to expect when processing the analytical components of my daily interaction with life. A voice from the past with which I could feel a strong connection, similar to what I once had when I was a little boy. It was as though I was speaking to myself from a slightly different perspective. Reminding me in a very subtle way that things weren't what they seemed to be.

This was extremely confusing as you can imagine. On the one hand, I was trying to sort out my newfound freedom as a young adult, while on the other, I felt this emptiness about my entire life. I couldn't shake this feeling that there was something superficial about the whole thing. As though my world wasn't real, or maybe I wasn't real. I found myself inexplicably drifting back to my youth and exploring the mysteries of my dreams in search of some meaning that could explain what was happening in my life.

It was there that I would surrender my fears for the sake of curiosity and an innocent obsession for the Truth. It would be this surrendering that would lead me down the path to understanding the meaning behind everything. It was there that I had my first metaphysical glimpse of an awakening that would not occur in my physical reality for another thirty years. Until then, I was at the mercy of the social construct, forcing its will upon me to accept its irrational logic for why things were the way they were.

Being raised a Catholic, I tried to rationalize the correlation between my lucid dreams and this increasing sense that I could be living in some sort of "dream state" in my outer reality. By giving it a religious interpretation, I came to the conclusion that somehow what I was experiencing had to be a "sign" from this thing I grew up knowing as God. That this God was somehow sending me a cryptic message as though I was chosen to do something with it. But for what purpose and why me?

For the longest time, I didn't want to see the world differently. I just wanted to live a normal life and do the normal things that everyone else was doing. But despite my efforts, the voice would find ways in which to remind me that things were not what they appeared to be. That somehow I had to connect all of this to my childhood dreams.

I would struggle with this puzzle for years, choosing to define my dreams within the context of a fear-based mentality. I used them to create an outer reality full of metaphorical demons disguised as everything and everyone. A reality so inconsistent with the true nature of my inner being that at times I found myself alone and utterly confused. I doubted even the beautiful things in my life, fearing that they too were somehow too good to be true. Another facet of my world that could, at any moment, be rendered obsolete. Yet, in my darkest moments I could sense the presence of a divine being, vigilantly standing within and all around me.

Though there were times I would face the Truth in my twenties and thirties, it wasn't until my mid-forties that its calling could no longer be ignored. At which time, I began what I refer to as the greatest odyssey of my life. An odyssey that would involve the most daring adventure inward to discover my true authenticity, never dreaming I would discover the path to my soul. I would later describe this adventure as my "Inner Quest" for Truth. An amazing quest full of imagination and intrigue where I could escape into a world of infinite possibilities.

As time went on, my outer world became less relevant to me. Though I would be lying if I said this happened overnight. But when I finally realized it's true purpose, my physical reality began to take on a more magical quality in my life. I started to see it for the playground that it was, a world full of infinite dreams.

To get there though would not be easy. I would have to come to grips with my inner demons and my emotional addiction to the negative aspects of my life. An addiction meant to keep me in submission in order to play out my role as victim in the dream state. I would call this segment of my odyssey the "Outer Journey," referring to my struggles to accept that the physical reality I was led to believe in was simply a dream which I had been asleep in since birth.

I was in my early fifties when it dawned on me that what was happening in my life was analogous to my lucid dreams. That these demons were no different than those that would haunt me as a child. That they weren't there to drown me in fear but rather to remind me to wake up. It would become one of the greatest epiphanies in my life that would ultimately lead to my permanent awakening. Moreover, my fears were a gift – a wakeup call if you will – that I had given myself as a reminder of how to overcome the transformation of the dream state. For the first time in my life I felt free again.

"So what is the purpose of the dream state?" you will ask. "And, why does it seem as though things are changing now within it?" The simple answer is that the dream state is unique to this time-space reality. It is a three dimensional reality that vibrates at a very low frequency. I introduce the term "frequency" right now because as I have already stated, everything exists as energy. Since energy is infinite, everything that is possible is happening in some dimension of frequency we simply cannot experience with our five senses.

Now here is where things get a little tricky for the analytical mind to rationalize. As God, it has always been our desire to experience our true Self in every way imaginable. One way to do so, is to introduce the element of contrast into the equation thereby giving us the ability to view our authenticity by creating the illusion or dream of what we are not. So what are we?

That too is simple to explain. In the purest sense of it all, we are the most magnificent interpretation of unconditional love we could ever imagine existing. Everything that radiates from us is some facet of love expressing itself as God energy. Admittedly, I find it almost difficult to describe because the feeling is unlike anything we have ever experienced with our physical senses. The only reason I know these feelings exist is because of a near death experience that would later in life trigger a remembrance of being in that light. As I would later describe, it felt like a million hugs. A feeling of unimaginable bliss so intense I didn't want it to end.

I came to understand the importance of the dream state within the context of that remembrance. I realized that if I had known no contrast at the time, I could not have appreciated the beauty and authenticity of who I was as God expressing myself in this human existence. In other words, it made that experience that much greater by giving it a point of reference that only contrast could give it. That would go for every aspect of love I could imagine. For instance, to fully appreciate myself as love, why not create the illusion of fear? To fully experience joy, why not create sadness? To delight in faith, why not introduce doubt? And to know myself as God, why not experience the ego?

All of this was done so that we as God could fully appreciate the brilliance of our divinity, which in turn, would expand our awareness of our spiritual infinity. In other words, it allows us as God to expand no differently than how our universe is growing limitlessly. Or, how we as individual divinity are growing in each moment of our Now. In fact, everything that is happening in our physical reality is simply a reflection of our awareness that as consciousness we are also expanding.

The dream state has allowed me to play out a game of discovery and remembrance. To be more precise, it is a game that has created an earth bound existence that is analogous to what we would know as a "school" experience. I will talk about this earthly experience in greater detail later in the book, but for now I want to briefly discuss its significance relative to the evolution of the dream state over the past several millennium.

In the beginning, the dream state had very limited parameters, for God's only intention was to experience itself through us from a conscious state of awareness known as duality. During this time, a select few would seek out and find their true awakening. A phenomenon that would cause an entire social construct to be formed. Teachings that would give rise to religions whose institutions would weave their spiritual fabric into the creation of both the western and eastern civilizations of our time.

We are now at a point in our spiritual evolution whereby the dream state, as it was originally intended, serves very little purpose. And thus, it too is evolving so that we as God may continue to grow in our awareness and appreciation of ourselves. This process has existed for thousands of years, but it wasn't until recently that we chose to introduce an entirely new element whereby we as Consciousness would awaken to the realization that something is co-existing with what we know as the physical. That individually, we would begin to see an entirely new story unfolding that would draw us inward toward the Truth.

The new dream state is designed to expand our awareness that indeed we are asleep. A new reality with new experiences was being born. We as God had achieved everything we had set out to do in the original dream state. Every expression of ourselves as contrast was explored a million times over. The game had lost its brilliance. It was time to move on.

It would be here that we would find adventure and intrigue. Solving the mystery of our existence as divinity experiencing itself individually in this physical reality. Consequently, many more would come to seek out their true identity. And along the way, the new dream state would offer clues, signs, or as I would call them "defining moments" in our quest for the Truth.

In recent times, the unfolding has presented itself to many and more are seeing the signs for what they were meant to show. The game is accelerating as if to reach some cosmic climax or maybe yet, another reality. But this reality is meant to be experienced in a far more awakened state of consciousness. A state of consciousness that is no longer limited to the conditions of this time-space reality. An awakened state where we no longer view ourselves as limited but expansive. Where we dare to experience ourselves as greatness beyond measure.

This calling to greatness will be discussed further in subsequent chapters, but for now know that it is not an illusion or as some might have you think – a delusion of grandeur. It is simply who we are and will forever be. It is simply an awakened state of our true beauty and power as God being God. We do not need to fear it nor should we ever feel unworthy of it. We simply have to believe it, understand it, expect it and become it.

Consequently, many who have awakened have begun to question, if not entirely abandon, their belief systems in the name of taking back their spiritual identity. And though I applaud this bravery, there still seems to be something missing. As if a clue has been overlooked which has led many, including yours truly, to struggle mightily with any effort to stay awake.

For years, I would labor to reconcile this new found spiritual freedom with the demons of my past. I would revert to my analytical ways as though somehow that aspect of my consciousness held the secret to unlocking this mystery. I would search for answers outwardly expecting things to change despite doing nothing to change my inner reality. As such, each day brought the same habitual behavior to my life. As in the movie *Groundhog Day,* my life had become an endless loop playing back the events of my previous day.

As with the character in that movie, I refused to see the obvious signs in front of me. It took a desperate plea for help to finally see the Truth. "And what would that be?" you will ask. That we have never been trapped in the dream state. Ultimately, we are meant to understand its playful nature and to treat it for the game that it is. That nothing is holding us back from realizing this Truth other than ourselves. That if we could just get out of our own way, we would see that the dream state is simply here to show us the way back to ourselves. To wake up to who we really are as individual expressions of God.

Sometimes these moments can be so minute that you may not even notice, much less appreciate them for their brilliance. Other times, they are meant to be very obvious and leave a lasting impression; as if their intent was to shock you into remembering. Regardless of their intensity, they are your most dependable companions pushing you relentlessly toward your awakening. "But what if I don't have any defining moments?" you will ask. Rest assured, you have all had such moments. However, if you insist on believing you have not, then make this moment, make this book – your defining moment! The moment your inner voice spoke to you in a way that you have never been spoken to before.

As you awaken, you will remember those signs or defining moments you overlooked in life. I know I did. I have had so many that if I were to write them down they would fill up a room. To this day, I am amazed at how obvious they should have been and how abundantly they flowed into my life. Rarely does a week go by that I don't recall yet another moment where the signs were so blatant. If only I would have seen them for what they were rather than what others had taught me to believe. Yet, there are no regrets, for I know that everything has unfolded perfectly to get me to this precise moment in my life.

Though I will share with you several of these defining moments within the context of what I will discuss later, for now I would like to share two. Moments that were so significant that I later attribute them as having been the catalyst for coming out to both myself and the world as a *Closet Spiritualist.* It is my desire that by sharing these moments, you will come to remember not only your moments, but the true meaning behind them as well.

> *I was born in Bogota, Colombia in what I would describe as a middle-class family. As was customary in those days, my parents were raised to be devout Catholics. Well, more exactly my mother was the devout one. Her faith in God could have moved mountains if only she had known how. And yet, that faith would play an enormous role, not long after my birth, in setting the course for my spiritual awakening years later.*
>
> *At six months, I came down with pneumonia. I was taken to the hospital for precautionary measures but within hours of being admitted my condition had*

worsened. As valiantly as they tried, the doctors knew that it was simply a matter of time before I would succumb to its wishes. They called for the chaplain and gathered the family to tell them the somber news that I had only hours to live.

My mother would later tell me that when she heard the news, her body went limp. A sense of absolute disbelief came over her. The room went dark and lifeless and the voices became distant, as if she were being pulled away into a dream. But just then, an intense energy engulfed her that simply would not let her go. It wasn't one of fear or immense sadness, but rather one of unshakable faith, determination and love.

Upon feeling its presence she immediately got down on her knees, shook off her physical reality, began praying in a deeply meditative state, and crawled to the nearest church a block away. I use the term "meditative" because she never asked God for anything, but rather she thanked God for the time she had been given to experience my light in this world. She was eternally grateful and appreciative of every moment she had had with me up until then.

Without knowing it, her focus drifted from her past to her future. She saw me growing up and becoming this wonderful man. A loving son, a devoted husband and father, and caring human being. She was filled with an overwhelming sense of love at what she was experiencing. It was as though she was there living that moment with me. She remembers describing it to God as if she were "willing" me to stay alive and experience this future. She would later tell me that it was impossible for her to see a world void of my light. It just did not exist in her reality.

She was overcome with tears of joy. Any sadness or fear had disappeared. Her heart was full of love and gratitude as a blanket of peacefulness draped her from head to toe. It was at that point that she knew, without a doubt, that everything in her physical reality had changed. Without having to be told, she knew in her heart that things were going to be alright. That I would live and grow up to be the man she envisioned in her prayers.

She immediately went back to the hospital where she was welcomed with tearful hugs by family and hospital staff alike. The doctors would later describe what happened that day as nothing less than a miracle. An act of God that defied medical reasoning. For in the time that she was gone, I went from having a near death experience to a full recovery, showing no signs of pneumonia at all.

On that day, my mother moved a mountain for me. Though she would never come to realize the enormity of her act as God, she left a trail of bread crumbs for me to do so later in life. A tremendous act of selfless love that only a mother could have for her child. A bond so pure and innocent that it would cause the universe to bow before its presence and give her the miracle she desired.

I was in my late teens when I came to learn about my near death experience. But it would be years later before I would see the true meaning behind this moment. When I did, however, it would form the cornerstone of my spiritual belief system. For you see it wasn't about the miracle or whether I would go on to do wondrous things in my life, it was about her. It was about her faith, determination and love and how these three attributes not only held the secret by which to wake up from the dream state, but also the ability to manifest an entirely new reality. I cannot stress the enormity of what was just said, so please take a moment to let it sink in, and if need be – read it over and over, until it does.

> *Fast forward and I am now thirty-seven. My wife Sharlene and I had just become parents for the second time and since my career was going well, she and the kids were able to join me on a business trip to Phoenix for a month. Upon landing, we decided that the best course of action would be for me to bring the rental car over and meet them curbside since we had so much to carry.*
>
> *Unfamiliar with the airport, I took the outer lane designed to let traffic flow freely for those who were bypassing the arrival area. Unfortunately, that lane would take me away from where Sharlene would come out, leaving me to park by an island designated for passengers seeking public transportation.*
>
> *Just then, I saw Sharlene navigating her way through the sliding doors. Savannah in her car seat in one hand and Logan holding on playfully to the other. I yelled to draw her attention but only Logan could hear me. As with any two year old, his immediate response was to throw caution to the wind and scurry over to be by my side.*
>
> *A sense of horror overcame me as I saw a stream of cars racing toward him. There was no way I would*

reach him in time since I was at least 100 feet away. I knew he had only seconds to live if something wasn't done. But what could I do? I was too far away and Logan was already sprinting across three lanes of oncoming traffic. And then it happened.

A voice deep within moved quickly to gather every bit of energy in me to summon the one thing I knew to do instinctively as a parent. I screamed, "No!" with such intensity that its reverberation would cause me to witness something whose explanation would defy any conventional logic or wisdom of our day.

At that moment everything stopped. I mean everything – the cars, people, the airplanes and even the external noise around me. The intensity was like a tsunami crushing everything in its path. But if that wasn't enough, without notice I found myself in the back seat of the car that was directly in Logan's path. I was yelling at the driver, a young lady in her early twenties, to "stop" which caused her to immediately slam on the breaks and go crashing into the steering wheel. The thing is that in my physical reality, I wasn't anywhere near her and yet her car would come to a screeching halt some 125 feet away.

But it gets even more bizarre. A second later, I was standing outside again by the rental car watching as the energy of my voice created a massive ripple effect upon the landscape of my physical reality. It was as if my entire vista was being projected on a transparent screen that was waving effortlessly in the wind. A movie that was playing all around me and whose

> *physical properties went from three-dimensional to two-dimensional and then back to three in a split second.*
>
> *When it was all done, everything went back to "normal." In a blink of an eye, there was Logan running harmlessly across the street as traffic would come to a slow and uneventful halt. The drivers just gathered themselves for a moment and went on their way as if nothing had really happened. In fact, everything went back to normal in a somewhat eerie manner leaving me to ask, "What the hell just happened?"*

Looking back, I didn't care to know the answer. I was just happy that my son was alive. But it wouldn't take long before I would begin to replay the events of that day over and over again. Like my lucid dreaming, that day would leave a lasting impression that would haunt me for years.

Inevitably, I knew I would have to face the Truth of what happened that day. A Truth I simply was not ready to handle. Years later, when I was ready to trust the voice within, I would come to realize that an extraordinary shift in reality had occurred that day. That for some reason, I was given an opportunity to see how the universe operated from both a metaphysical and quantum physical perspective. Neither of which I knew anything about at the time. Like Dorothy in *The Wizard of Oz,* I was shown the Truth as to the secrets behind the mystical curtain of my extraordinary world.

Being a creature of the analytic mind, I would seek to validate the epiphanies I would have from this experience through a wealth of findings made in so many areas of science. I was absolutely astonished to find that no matter what set of lenses I would look through, the Truth remained the same. That this Truth went way beyond science into the fields of mathematics, religion, philosophy, history, archeology and so many other disciplines. Consequently, there is so much to share, but for now know that this incident opened my eyes to the holographic Truth of our physical reality. An awareness so profound that it would mark the beginning of my Outer Journey and the subsequent end to the physical identity I once knew as myself.

Chapter Three

The Outer Journey

Long ago, before time existed, humanity knew itself as God. It understood and could feel that the connection with everything began with knowing itself as everything. Concepts that kept us separated such as time and space, past and future and even life and death did not exist the way we perceive them to be today. It was by all accounts a blissful state of beingness. Yet, one that offered little to no contrast by which to grow as God.

In our desire to experience ourselves as something new we chose to forget our spiritual identity; thus, a region of our mind went dormant, giving way to a veil of chaotic energy that has kept us in a state of suspended living until now. Our inability to remember forced us to observe the world from a limited sense of consciousness. What many of you have come to know as the ego construct. The significance of this consciousness cannot be stated enough, for its intention was to have us react to life as if things were happening to us from somewhere *out there*, rather than to go searching for answers deep within the stillness of our mind.

To ensure our focus would be kept *out there*, we created institutions with rigid structures and procedures to guide our every thought from birth. The foundation of these institutions would be fear-based, designed to challenge our every move. As if to leave no stone unturned, we implanted worthless programing within ourselves inhibiting our ability to grow spiritually; leaving us with an apathetic willingness to discover the Truth.

As children, we agreed to the social conditioning of those who influenced us the most. People who meant well and loved us dearly but who had long forgotten their beingness. They simply lacked the spiritual maturity to guide us into the future. We accepted their conditioning as "normal" and quickly adopted them as our own.

By the time we reached our teens, our conditioning had become part of our energetic frequency. An unwelcomed element to our spiritual identity. Once engraved, we were destined to play out the original dream state by exhibiting the same pathological behaviors as everyone else. Those that managed to stay awake, however, were left to wander aimlessly for answers; social outcasts to the world and often to themselves.

As adults, we would spend our time chasing life the way a dog would chase its tail. Going around and around, never really getting anywhere that could bring us peace, love, happiness and spiritual freedom. Being so disconnected from ourselves, we would blame others for our lot in life. And when all else would fail, we would blame ourselves for our insecurities.

We created a social construct designed to keep us amused by inventing ways in which to distract us from the Truth. We became obsessed with any and all forms of external gratification despite the shallowness of their substance. Religions that were once formed to create a sense of community among like-minded individuals would come to be used as a means by which to hold salvation in the hands of the faceless few. Creating a subservient state of beings fearful that their actions here on earth could one day influence their chance at spiritual immortality.

Our political systems would do a masterful job of hiding the Truth by having us point fingers at each other for the problems in our lives. All while succumbing to the demands of our educational systems which would require us to go through regimental schooling aimed at creating a social class of obedient consumers and workers beholden to the ruling elite. Not to be outdone, our financial institutions would hold us captive, lusting over a monetary system that has no real value other than the one it serves for the privileged few. Reminding us at every turn that true happiness, if not one's survival, was dependent upon our ability to achieve a certain level of financial success.

If those weren't enough, the so-called connections we created through advancements in technology and the internet, were at best, shallow and lacking in any real substance. Our social media platforms offer no meaningful connectivity to humanity, much less the spiritual beingness of our planet. Though hundreds of millions, if not billions of people wide, humanity's connection to one another is only inches deep and getting thinner at an alarming rate.

Though perfect in its intention, the world of duality has now run its course. As spiritual beings we are being called to graduate from this earthly existence to enjoy new experiences as God. In doing so, we are to transcend this world and enter into a new state of consciousness. One that is aligned with the higher frequencies of who we are as spiritual beings. It is not that we will leave this external world, but rather we come to experience it in a higher state of vibration that can only be described as "Heaven on Earth." Which brings me to where we are now – a world transitioning between vibrational realities.

Today, there exists two dominant forms of consciousness, each offering a different perspective to our physical reality. There is the Left Brain Consciousness whose analytical perception of life we believe to be reality; and the Right Brain Consciousness whose experiential reality of life we believe to be perception. The former is where the overwhelming majority of humanity still resides. The latter represents the awakened state of beingness that begins within the new dream state. It is this consciousness that we have come here to experience so that others might wake up as well.

Like everyone else, I have experienced duality to the fullest. As far back as I can remember, I was taught that peace existed *out there*. Love existed *out there*. Happiness existed *out there*. That to get what I wanted relative to these three, I would need to find it *out there*. As such, I would spend my life frantically searching for answers *out there*, never considering the possibility that they might already exist within me. I did this in every aspect of my life, including my most cherished relationship with God. I was told that God existed somewhere *out there* in a place I could neither see nor feel. And the worse thing was – I believed it!

I sought comfort in a God reigning from some heavenly kingdom by which only death would give me right to its passage. A God who would appear only to the chosen few. Whose voice I could never hear and whose love I could only wish for. But why? Why would anyone, much less God, behave so irrationally? Thankfully, I would come to discover the Truth to that question in my mid-teens. Though only a glimpse, it would lay the groundwork by which my opinion of an external God would change my life forever.

> *At fifteen, I was lost in my own spiritual abyss, seeking answers "out there" to quench my soul. I would see beauty in others only to question my worthiness in*

its presence. My inner world had become a foreign wasteland. Unbeknownst to me, I had fallen prey to the original dream state I knew nothing of.

Unable to find my own answers, I did everything I could to adhere to the social construct in the hopes that by playing its game I would find happiness and purpose in my life. My world became an endless journey of contradiction with no rational way to explain it all. The more I relied on external conditions for peace, love, happiness and spiritual freedom, the further away they would get. I looked for every external means by which to achieve gratification, and when those wells would dry up, I would go searching for more.

One night, I was lying in bed shaking uncontrollably with fear. My heart was so heavy that I broke down in tears. In desperation, I called out to God for clarity and comfort. I hung on desperately to my pillow as wave after wave of emotions came crashing across the bow of my fragile existence. My prayers grew in intensity for what seemed like hours until I could feel the heaviness disappear as fear gave way to fatigue. I took advantage of the moment to close my eyes and breathe again, hoping that sleep would come to my rescue.

It felt like only seconds had gone by when I began to experience this unusual sense that my body was drifting away somewhere. Since I slept on the top bunk bed, I was convinced that I had somehow rolled over to the edge and was now free falling to the floor.

Instead, I opened my eyes, only to find myself standing in the middle of some desert.

I looked down and to my surprise I saw an old, decrepit man reaching out as if he were begging for something – maybe money or food. But he wasn't looking at me, he was looking through me. His eyes were absorbed in something way beyond me. I turned to look up, only to see this beautiful orb radiating a warmth I had never felt before. Though considerably larger than the sun, its light was gentle to my eyes, allowing me to stare directly at it.

I looked down to see that the old man had disappeared and in his place was this frail, young boy. He too was reaching out for something that only the light could give him. I looked up again, only to find that the orb was now coming toward me. I was completely mesmerized, helplessly drifting toward a light that would soon engulf me. Yet, I felt no fear, for its beauty was overwhelming and its love too intoxicating. In seconds, it had weaved its way into every cell of my body, leaving each to vibrate uncontrollably in its wake.

Once inside, I was astounded to see that this magnificent orb was made up of individual silhouettes whose beingness would become clear to me as they drew closer. I felt an incredible connection to these angelic beings as if somehow I had known them forever. What happened next would leave a profound imprint on my life that I would carry to this day.

As they came closer, I knew they were there to welcome me home. The joy I felt from their embrace was beyond description. I have never felt such love in my life. It was as though every cell was vibrating with such intensity that at any moment I would explode. And yet, there was this peaceful sense of Oneness that was everywhere because I was everywhere. There was no beginning nor end to my essence. I had become part of the light, both the receiver and the giver. It was endless and I didn't want it to stop. But just then – it did!

I felt what I could only describe as an "out-of-body" experience as this hand pulled me away from the light just when I was ready to surrender to its rapture. In seconds, I was plummeting toward my physical reality with such velocity that its impact would wake me up gasping for air as if I had been submerged in water for minutes. I was back. Back in a world I did not want to be in.

Just then, I felt this peaceful presence all around me. I could sense that there was something different about my world. That this feeling of unconditional love had come back with me as if to remind me that I was more than this physical reality – a keepsake of my brief encounter with Oneness. A feeling that spoke to me in a language only my heart could hear. A language that I would come to remember as I got much older and less resistant to the Truth.

I laid in bed for hours fully awake to this feeling. Tears of joy and gratitude filled my heart as I knew I had experienced something beyond this earthly existence. It was the first of many encounters I would have whose purpose would be to remind me that the world I believed to be real, was in fact the true perception of my reality.

It would be years before I would peel back the secrets behind this beautiful vision. I would call this vision my "Million Hugs," grateful for the glimpse it gave me of a reality most could not conceive. Going forward, I would choose to focus my attention simply on the hugs; longing for their blissfulness, if only for a moment. A reality where I was inseparable from God because I "was" God. A reality where my capacity for love and my connection with everything was infinite because I too was infinite.

I cannot count how many times this vision would come to my rescue. How many times the memory of those hugs would pull me away from the shadows of my outer world. How many times they would serve to remind me that the real dream was *out there*, and that something was calling me to explore my inner world for the Truth. This vision would become my beacon, navigating me home through the troubled waters of my dream state. Reminding me to stay the course because the journey *out there* wasn't to be feared, but rather enjoyed like a game of *Connect the Dots.*

More importantly, this vision inspired me to remember that the things most cherished are not obtainable in the physical, but rather within each and every one of us! That before anything ever was, I Am. Therefore, I Am is peace, I Am is love, and I Am is happiness. We have, and always will be, everything to all. This is the most profound message that everyone, from the greatest spiritual minds to those who have had near death experiences, have attempted to share with all of humanity.

I owed it to myself to find the courage to decipher this vision. To discover the meaning behind its meaning in the hope that I would see the obvious. But like most, I simply refused to do anything to change the circumstances of my life. Instead, I would take the path of least resistance and wallow in my misery; seeking whatever gratification the social construct would give. Willingly giving away my soul for the chance to live what I thought was a normal life.

It would take the words of a stranger to wake me from my state of denial. To show me, yet again, my true identity as a spiritual being living a human existence with a specific purpose for being here at this time. A purpose which I was unwilling to accept, much less share with anyone other than Sharlene. One that would rock my world and send me plummeting down the proverbial rabbit hole of my life.

> *A year after the airport incident, I was at a summer solstice party hosted by an acquaintance who lived in the neighborhood. It was a beautiful night and to be honest, a bit magical in its appearance. This person was known to be a bit eccentric so it didn't surprise me that he had hired a psychic to perform readings for his guests. Somewhat skeptical, but mostly scared, I reluctantly agreed to have my fortune read.*
>
> *I went upstairs and joined a line of people who were anxiously awaiting their turn. One by one they filed in, and then in almost predictable fashion, they would walk out sobbing. Almost to a person, they were overwhelmed by the accuracy within which this psychic knew about their lives or those of their loved ones, deceased or alive.*
>
> *When it was my turn, I sat down and was prepared to hear the same. I kept telling myself that this psychic*

wasn't going to get the best of me, so I sat there prepared for battle. She welcomed me and asked that I remain silent as she waited for some message to come through. Within seconds, my fear had subsided giving way to a light-hearted giggle as I could not help but see the humor in what I was doing.

Just as I was ready to settle in, the energy in the room changed. Her eyes opened widely as if something had jolted her into a state of disbelief. She took hold of my hands as her eyes fixated on mine with a penetrating focus I had seen many times before and would see again later in life. Her voice intensified as the word "I" was replaced by "we" in her vocabulary.

"You're not from here, are you?" she asked, as her voice took on a much deeper tone. "You've traveled a long way to get here," she proceeded, not waiting for an answer. Naïve to what was happening, I jumped in and told her that I was from Chicago, though I never thought it to be that far from Minneapolis. I wasn't trying to be funny and luckily she didn't take it that way.

She looked at me with such extreme gratitude as she explained how I had come from some other place in time having mastered this world many lifetimes ago. That I had come here to bring forth an idea that would change the world. Like a mantra, she just kept repeating her vision as her eyes began to fill up with tears.

I was in a state of shock. The house could have burned down at that moment but it wouldn't have mattered to me. Tears of joy were streaming down her cheek as she thanked me for choosing to come back to share my light.

As strange as this might sound, I felt an immediate connection to her and the entity she was channeling. I knew then and there that this life of normality I had tried so desperately to maintain was about to come crashing down on me. For the first time in my life, I felt an alarm go off inside forcing me to confront forgotten memories that were now cascading through my mind. Memories whose signs I had refused to acknowledge throughout my life.

Somehow, I mustered up enough courage to ask if we were done. It's not that I really wanted it to end, but I just could not bear to hear more of what I already knew. My words must have jolted her enough because she sat up immediately and with her hands now on her heart, she began to whisper what sounded like a chant. "We thank you for being here – thank you, thank you so much!" she repeated, as she rocked back and forth in her chair.

I collected myself as best as I could and walked out the door. I managed to make it down the stairs and into the backyard where I would eventually meet up with Sharlene. As I laid there on the grass, I couldn't stop hearing her voice nor could I stop thinking about the expression on her face as she stared right through me. Speaking not to the physical me but the spiritual essence within me.

I felt like a raft that had been set adrift in a raging hurricane. It took everything in me to pull myself together and move on with my life. I know that may seem a bit extreme but my faith at that time was already in shambles. I did not need some psychic to make it worse. And yet, as much as I tried to downplay what had happened, I knew she had lit a fire within me. A fire that would slowly ignite an awakening that was still seven years in the making.

Over the next several years, my life would teeter between perception and reality. To be honest, I often had a hard time differentiating between the two. There would be other events whereby my spiritual identity would be exposed to my fragile ego. Where I would see the subtle cracks in the walls of my physical reality. Most would be remarkably similar relative to both the story itself and the circumstances that would lead to some stranger revealing my true identity.

I recall an incident at a restaurant once where I struck up a conversation with someone I had just met. I was waiting for some friends to arrive so I thought I would order a drink at the bar. I didn't think much of it but I found myself making small talk with the gentleman next to me.

At one point, I recall pontificating about all sorts of things – politics, religion, humanity's plight, etc. Nothing very deep but it helped to pass the time away. About thirty minutes into the conversation something rather bizarre happened. For no apparent reason the gentleman's demeanor took an inexplicable turn right before my eyes. His voice turned raspy as he stopped in mid-stream of an entirely different thought and began to prophesize the things I would do in my life.

His story was remarkably similar to the one I heard at the summer solstice. He too would have the same expression of gratitude on his face as he looked at me with eyes that were speaking to someone other than me. He grabbed me by the elbows and would not let go, as if he knew I would leap from my chair the moment I had a chance to escape. His eyes began to tear up as if he were desperately trying to get a message across that I simply wasn't getting.

I remember looking around for help but no one seemed to notice. People were just going about their evening as if we no longer existed in the room. It was such a surreal experience. I felt as though I had entered some sort of dream state where everything around me was moving in slow motion.

I was speechless, not just because of the events that were unfolding before me, but because of the voice that was projecting through him. It wasn't his, for I had heard this voice many times before. I had heard it in my dreams as a child and in my darkest moments in life when I was searching for comfort. It was the voice that was present in my Million Hugs and would be there again at the airport when I shouted out to save Logan. A voice I knew from somewhere long ago. A companion from some other place and time.

I felt a jolt that brought everything back into the moment. It was as if someone had snapped their fingers and everyone woke up again. Just like that,

> *the conversation went back to what it was before. The gentleman made his original point, took a drink from his glass and looked away as if to say he was done socializing. The timing could not have been better since my friends had just walked in and within seconds we were being seated at a table.*

Like the summer solstice party, it took everything in me to move on. To shake things off and call what happened that night a fluke of some kind even though I knew better. Deep within me there was something happening in my life I was deathly afraid to acknowledge, but being young and naïve I just went on pretending as if it didn't really matter. Suffice it to say it did matter. It mattered so much that my perception of reality was being called into question at every turn.

Why were these events happening in my life? Why were so many things not adding up? And why was I having this irresistible urge to retrace my steps as if there were clues hidden in the puzzle I knew as my past? Clues that would help me to understand why I was beginning to see the world so differently, and more importantly, why others could not.

Nevertheless, I kept marching on. On the surface you wouldn't even know that a war was waging within me. A cry for help as I tried to make sense of it all within the limits of my social conditioning. Like most, I would spend my days adhering to a set of rigid behaviors that I could perform in my sleep. The irony was that I was asleep and I didn't even know it.

As with my lucid dreams, something or someone was trying to wake me up to the Truth, but I simply refused to do so. For me, it was too easy to maintain the status quo. Too easy to look to others for answers to my problems. Too easy to curl up and accept the role life had given me as the victim of my reality.

By the time I reached my mid-forties, I was a ticking time bomb. I was struggling to get my newly-formed business off the ground but more importantly, I was struggling to get my life off the ground. I was lost in a world that I couldn't make sense of spiritually. For my family's sake, I went back to Catholicism as a way to anchor my children's faith at an early age. But after their baptism and a few makeshift Sunday school lessons at home, my desire to teach them about a God I did not even understand myself, waned quickly.

Instead, my days would be consumed by this burning desire to investigate the possibility that another reality was trying to reach out to me. A reality less foreign than the one I was living in. A world begging to be heard, for it possessed within itself, Truths to my spiritual identity. Nevertheless, fear would keep me from seeking out these Truths. In time, I found myself, once again, measuring my existence within the context of some outer expectations placed upon me by those representing the social construct. A set of expectations that were never meant to be fully achieved within the framework of the original dream state.

It would take yet another act of sheer desperation to wake up for the first time and experience a spiritual encounter that would bring me to my knees. An experience that would allow me to throw away my physical identity for the chance to know myself as something greater. A chance to find within me the peace, love, happiness and spiritual freedom I had been desperately searching for since childhood. A moment so incredible that it would mark the end of my original dream state and the beginning of my friendship with the Voice I would later come to know as Caleb.

Chapter Four

The Inner Quest

To me, the inner world has always been a place shrouded with mystery. A place I knew little of other than what I had been taught to believe through the social construct. A state of consciousness so abstract that it often held no relevance in my day-to-day interaction with life. Since birth, I was led to believe that nothing existed in my inner world other than the mind, which I presumed was way too analytical and rational for my taste. A consciousness highly motivated, if not controlled, by the ego construct. Therefore, implying that the two were somehow separate from one another.

Even my understanding of Spirit seemed to imply that it could not exist within the inner sanctums of my consciousness. That the two were somehow separated at birth. Secured in some dungeon deep within me, but whose location was a mystery to all. But what if the two are inseparable? What if the voice I was told not to listen to, much less speak to, was truly God? But not just any God, a higher version of me as God?

In the original dream state, to view yourself in such manner would be unheard of, bordering on blasphemy in the eyes of many religions. The mere act of talking to one's self would be cause for intervention since such behavior is often seen as disturbing, if not disruptive, to one's personal wellbeing. But who makes up these rules and by whose standards are they being measured against?

In the world of duality, there is always someone or something *out there* calling the shots. An entity of some kind that is determined to have us measure ourselves against one other in a desperate attempt to keep us distracted from the Truth. Filling us with nonsense that would have us think that the inner world is a sterile environment of the mind, and thus, a place unworthy of God.

To reinforce this belief, we create this being known as the ego construct whose job it is to deceive us at all cost. And when that's not enough, we create an even larger monster, known as the social construct, to cast as the villain in our play of life. But what if the inner world was actually a safe haven? A place to seek refuge from duality and the illusion we call our physical reality. I would imagine that for most, the idea of a refuge would seem to make some rational sense. But here is where the illusion of the original dream state must end, for the inner world is so much more than just a mere sanctuary of the mind.

It is here where I had to challenge myself to perceive beyond what I knew, and to imagine my inner world as the center of all reality. A reality whereby everything is consciousness, and therefore everything is life. As with every aspect of life, there is a stillness within its center whereby all creation is born. You see it in every element of nature, from the trillions of cells that make up our body, to the spiraling galaxies above. Close your eyes and know that as God, you "are" that stillness! It is you who is at the center of your universe because you are Consciousness. You are a living light of energy that knows itself as nothing and yet everything to all.

In other words, at the center of who you are, there exists only you as energy that goes on forever and ever. Expanding inward as you express yourself outwardly in physical form. If only you would permit yourself the experience of going inward as Consciousness, you would feel a silence so serene that its vibration could be felt throughout your body. That vibration is your soul who you have known consciously since you were a child. It speaks to you through a frequency of energy which goes way beyond our five senses. Though I assure you, it speaks to you in a language you were born to understand.

I know this sounds rather esoteric but it is not, for these Truths are being revealed within the new sciences of the day. The inner world is a magical place waiting to be explored, if only we would suspend our beliefs long enough to allow for such a possibility. It is the portal by which we will find ourselves again. Not as a physical being living a spiritual reality, but rather a spiritual being experiencing a physical reality.

It is deep within this portal that the voice, YOUR voice, patiently awaits your arrival. Patiently waiting to share the Truth of who you are and why you are here at this precise moment in time. It is this voice you hear right now as you contemplate whether to continue to deny yourself the life you came here to experience. The same voice that would come one fateful night when I could no longer bear the weight of my fragile existence.

> *At forty-five, I was a father of three beautiful children. My youngest, Sophia, was born seven years earlier. Sharlene had quit her job after Savannah was born to be a full-time, stay-at-home parent. We had a dog named Willie who came to us one Christmas Day*

and could not have been a more perfect fit for our family. On the surface, it was Americana at its finest. Something out of a "Norman Rockwell" painting.

Underneath it all, I was trying desperately to balance the extraordinary events of my past with the life I had created for my family. Unable to do so, I looked for signs everywhere that would validate my reasons for burying the Truth. I was determined to live a normal life knowing full well that I was living a lie.

One night, after putting my children to bed, a rush of hopelessness came over me. I had come to know this feeling all too well. It had become an unwelcomed companion whose presence in my life I simply could not avoid. I fell to my knees and began to cry uncontrollably. "Are you there?" I cried out in desperation. "I can't make any sense of my life. All I want is to go home, yet I don't even know what that means. If you can hear me, please send me a sign. I can't hang on much longer!" Not expecting an answer, I crawled into bed and cried myself to sleep. A habit I had become very good at.

The next morning, I woke up only to be greeted by my lonesome companion. "Did you not hear anything I said last night?" I would ask of the silence that lingered aimlessly in my mind. All along pressing my hands against my chest, unwilling to let go as if somehow that would provoke an answer. "I know you're here. I can sense you and I know you've tried to talk to me in the past. Why won't you say something?"

As determined as I was to wait for a reply, I could feel myself drifting into the stillness of my early morning slumber. I surrendered myself to its call, allowing it to take me to my next destination. It wasn't long before my senses were awakened as I found myself standing along a towering structure whose architecture, though unknown to me in this world, felt oddly familiar in a rather metaphysical way.

Without hesitation, I levitated to an open window high above. Inside, I could see that the building housed a circular library whose halls were adorned with magnificent marble and whose shelves were filled with books as far as the eye could see. I wandered over to a small collection of books that were perched several stories above the main entrance of the library. On the right hand side, two shelves from the top, I found what I had come for – a slightly worn, leather bound book thick with hundreds of pages that were ready for my exploration.

I opened the book and to my surprise the pages contained no words. Though puzzled at first, I knew intuitively what the book was asking me to do. I leaned over as if to bury my head. Just then, the pages began to glow and a voice emerged assuring me that there was nothing to fear. "Who are you?" I asked, somewhat rhetorically since I already knew the answer. "I am everything that is in you just as you are everything that is in me," the voice replied.

I laid there unshaken by the response. I had never heard such an explanation and yet, there was nothing more to be said. You see, I had felt its presence many times before, but this time I was open to whatever it had to say. In my heart, I was ready to experience what the book was there to reveal. Unbeknownst to me, what was about to be revealed would become the genesis for my first awakening and the inspiration for this book.

The knowledge that invaded my consciousness was incredible. It began with a glimpse of how humanity came to be and its relevance to the here and now. To be more precise, I was shown humanity's role relative to its symbiotic relationship with Gaia (i.e., Mother Earth), God and itself. Streams of data flowed effortlessly as the past gave way to the present and then the future. Almost as if all were happening simultaneously to each other, irrespective of time and space.

I was astonished by the massive amount of data I was downloading. I felt like a super computer as I inputted streams of data I knew nothing of, and yet it felt so natural to me. As if I knew exactly where it was going and how it needed to be processed. But just as I was making sense of it all, the transmission began to fade and I could feel myself reuniting with my body. Like my vision of the Million Hugs, I found myself drifting to a place I did not want to go back to.

I woke up to find that I had slept for about an hour. However, unlike the vision, I wasn't ready to settle for another nebulous dream that would leave me with more questions than answers. "No, you're not leaving

> *me this way!" I screamed hysterically in my mind. "What the hell is going on? I can't do this anymore. I need to understand why I'm being shown all this?"*
>
> *"Do not be afraid," the voice would say softly as a vibrational stream of images began to pour into my awaiting consciousness. My mind felt at home as I could sense that every neuron was being nourished with a gentle stream of energy I had never felt before.*
>
> *Thoughts of enlightenment filtered through my spiritual essence in the form of geometric patterns, equations and data bits. Though I did not understand their symbolic meaning, all I had to do was focus on one and a story would unfold. Stories whose lessons were not meant to teach, but rather to remind me of my spiritual identity and my purpose for being here to serve humanity.*
>
> *I remember feeling an overwhelming sense of humility and gratitude for what I had experienced that day. Finally, after years of fighting a needless battle, I was ready to wake up. I was ready to receive my calling and understand that I had nothing to fear. That it was time to experience my physical reality for what it was meant to be – a wonderland of infinite possibilities. Though I had no earthly idea where my voice would take me next, I was determined to hang on, for I knew deep down inside my life depended on it.*

The "Downloads" I received that day changed the course of my life forever. Like the transparent veil that was revealed at the airport years before, I realized that the Downloads were serving as some form of time capsule in which my higher Self was trying to reveal a story to me as Consciousness. A beingness that could somehow project itself onto a three-dimensional screen and call it reality.

Finally, I could feel that I had a much larger role to play in life and I couldn't wait to get started. No longer did I feel like a victim or prisoner to my reality, but rather as its architect or creator. Though I knew very little of my spiritual teachers, I began to sense a profound closeness to them that had never existed before. They were no longer these holy teachers from the past to be revered as deity, but rather long, lost family and friends who were waiting patiently to welcome me home. A home I had never left.

In their own way, they had walked this earth many times before. Sharing the Truth so that humanity could see its own perfection. They came here not to create religions that would ultimately distort their teachings, but rather to be a light to those seeking the most fundamental of all Truths – that before anything was, there was love whose light we have always been a part of. A state of beingness whose desire was to experience itself in all forms so that it could come to appreciate itself as nothing and everything to all. For without contrast, there would be no point of reference for it to know itself as Oneness.

Can you imagine the implications this would have on a world that lives completely separate from itself in every possible way? A world whose teachings are in direct opposition to everything being shown to you here. Going forward, I must warn you that everything you have been taught to believe about your outer reality will be challenged, for the inner world represents the only bastion of hope in your quest to liberate you from yourself.

The Truths that lie within you hold the key to unlocking the secrets behind the calling that has brought you here to this book, and to the life that awaits you once you have awakened. If you approach the remaining chapters from a place deep within your heart, you will come to unlock these secrets. But if you come with only your analytical mind, you will miss the messages hidden behind the words. You will see only what you have seen before, which is to say, you will walk away rationalizing that the quest for everything you desire is simply unattainable other than somewhere *out there*. In time, you will succumb to the lures of your outer reality, falling asleep and forgetting this experience ever happened. That is of course, until something or someone comes along to remind you that it is time to wake up again.

The Downloads would go on for several weeks and what they revealed to me was nothing less than extraordinary. Each time, taking me back to the same dream where I would find myself sitting in front of this wondrous book I would later know as the *Book of Life* or as some refer to it, the *Akashic Records.* At times, these Downloads would occur during the day simply by getting into a meditative state similar to a trance. The thing is, I knew nothing about meditation at the time, much less going into a trance, but somehow I knew what to do.

In each occurrence, I was greeted by my voice who would walk me through a specific "Knowing" held within the sacred pages of this book. I was shown how the original dream state came to be and our role in its creation. I was also shown the importance of the impending universal alignment of our galaxy and its role relative to the evolution of our consciousness in this time-space reality. I sat there mesmerized as I was reminded of the multi-dimensionality of the Now and the secret behind the "Divine DNA." The latter forming the geometric basis by which our physical reality is created. A triangular shape that is found in various ancient texts and traditions all over the world.

It would be years before this voice would share its name with me as Caleb. Caleb explained that to have done so any sooner would have created a relationship based on duality. A relationship whereby

I would view it as someone or something *out there* rather than my authentic Self or the consciousness within me.

> *"It was necessary for you to understand the essence of what we are before we would reveal ourselves to you by name," Caleb once told me. "The 'I Am' that is nothing and everything to all. You must first understand us as Oneness. That we are not bound by a name but rather a frequency of unconditional love. For you see, the 'I' represents the 'All' before anything was. Therefore, I Am in you and you are in me and together we create our reality."*

I am grateful for Caleb's wisdom, for it knew me better than I knew myself. By keeping our relationship as something I was experiencing with an inner voice, I would be forced to keep looking for answers deep within me. Answers that often seemed to have a sense of timeliness given the delicate state of my ego. But when they came, there was no mistaking their importance. Fragile or not, Caleb knew it was time for me to remember a specific Truth.

To that end, there are many more Truths you need to know that are relevant to your quest. They are to be used as tools to help you navigate the unchartered waters of your inner reality. Truths regarding misconceptions that have worked flawlessly within the original dream state, but whose value have no relevance in the new reality.

Illusions that were cleverly put there, by you, to limit your belief systems as if to dare you to enter at your own risk. Those that did, would find a world so dark and deceptively empty that its beauty could not be deciphered. The courageous few who ventured on would come to find a universe, so pristine, that its splendor would intoxicate the mind and awaken the soul.

It is in these Truths that the story of consciousness can be told. Like a rubber band, it will twist your mind so tightly that it will take everything in you to hold on as it unravels. Therefore, I will first explain what consciousness is not. Or shall I say, what you as "Consciousness" are not. To begin with, the "you" that you identify yourself to be as body DOES NOT EXIST! Your body is simply the physical expression or manifestation of who you view yourself to be as Consciousness. It is your avatar. A suit you wear to experience the physical reality you are creating in your mind. It only exists because you "believe" it to exist!

Therefore, you are not confined to your body, but rather it is confined to you. It is the first layer of your physical manifestation. A physical signature or reflection of who you are as a vibrational being. In either dream state, your body serves to remind you as to when you have deviated from your inner alignment with your higher Self. It does so by creating blockages that appear as unpleasant emotions which eventually manifest into symptomatic conditions you know as physical or mental illness, disease, pain or discomfort.

The world beyond your body is also an extension of who you are as Consciousness. It is as much your body as the one you see in the mirror every day. It responds to you as Consciousness in precisely the same manner. Therefore, it can create similar blockages in your physical world that appear as symptomatic conditions of life. If you view yourself in a negative light, I assure you that the world around you will manifest itself in a similar way. You will be bombarded with negativity everywhere you go. I will talk more about this in subsequent chapters. For now, know that you are pure, vibrational energy whose physical reality revolves around you as its beacon of light.

There are three forms of consciousness that operate within your mind. Together they form every aspect of your reality. The obvious question you will ask yourself is, "Which consciousness am I?" I will caution you that if asked in this manner, the question will never reveal the Truth. For you see, Consciousness exists only as Oneness. It is only in the dream state that we believe it exists in multiple forms. Therefore, the answer is that you are all Consciousness – all the time! You just don't know it.

I have alluded to two of these consciousness, but I will now offer an explanation of each within the context of your inner world. The first is the Left Brain Consciousness. It is the consciousness that we are most familiar with as it has guided our every thought since birth. It is the rational, analytical and tactical elements of the mind. In other words, it is the operating system of the soul. It uses reason as its programming language which oversees all the background components that enable us to create our reality.

In the metaphysical world, its role is to interpret the energetic signals of the five senses. Therefore, when the original dream state was formed and all other areas of the mind were forgotten, the Left Brain Consciousness was left to create a world void of the experiential energies that give meaning to life. The result was a world that appeared to be far from perfect, but in the original dream state that was exactly our intention. A world in which two plus two often equaled five. Forcing us to accept its absurd explanations as to why such occurrences could exist.

The physical manifestations of the Left Brain Consciousness are most prevalent in the structural identity of our world. You see it everywhere from the laws we have written to the moral and ethical codes we stand by. It is not that these in-and-of themselves are wrong, but rather in how expansive they have become in dictating our every thought and action. Laws and codes that were left to be created by those whose faces and names we know little of and who exist somewhere *out there*.

Though it is not required that you understand its mechanical function as it relates to the creative process, I would like to share with you a simple overview. As such, know that whenever energy is interpreted by our physical senses, a signal is sent to the etheric pathways of the mind. Pathways that are independent of, but still located in and around the left hemisphere of the brain. Like a processor, the signal is then interpreted by the Left Brain Consciousness as an outer experience and a thought is created that reaffirms that reality.

Thought then acts as its own energetic signal, which is then carried to the lower chakra regions of the body where an intention – based on either love or fear – is created and sent to the heart chakra. The heart chakra then translates the intention and emotes an electromagnetic field we know as feelings. Inwardly, these feelings cause the neural pathways of the body to release chemicals that define the genetic expression of our cells. In other words, our bodies become the physical manifestation of our thoughts and emotions.

Outwardly, the same process is also taking place. A process that will be discussed in greater detail later in the book. For now, know that our feelings form the experiential language by which we speak to the Universe in creating our physical reality. As science is now discovering, the entire universe is connected by a neural system that is remarkably similar to ours. And since we are all energy, we are all connected to the same system. Therefore, we are all co-creating our world through the thoughts and emotions of our etheric mind. *(see Figs. 4.1 through 4.3).*

Left Brain Consciousness

Translation of Energy in Creating Your "Outer" Reality

Figure 4.1

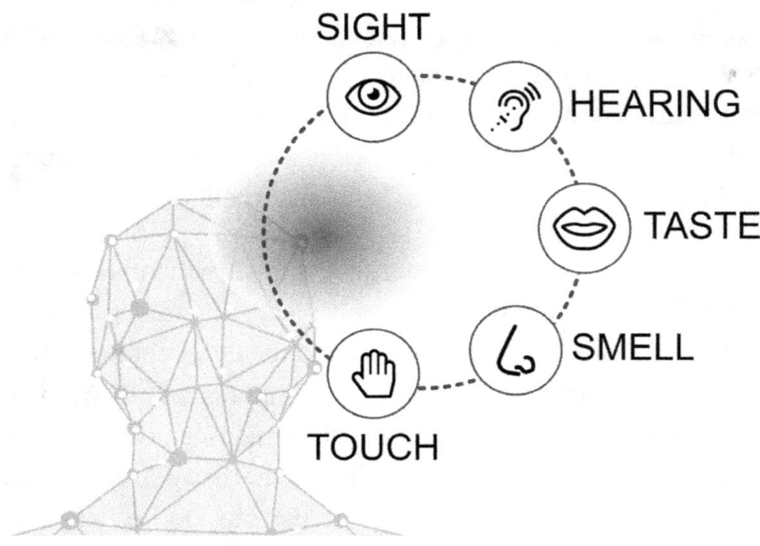

3rd Dimension of Physical Reality

In the original dream state, energy is interpreted by the five physical senses and an energetic signal is sent to the etheric pathways of the analytical mind known as the Left Brain Consciousness (LBC). The LBC resides in and around the left hemisphere of the brain but is completely independent of it. The signals are interpreted by the LBC as an outer experience and are reaffirmed by the creation of a thought.

Left Brain Consciousness

Translation of Energy in Creating Your "Outer" Reality

Figure 4.2

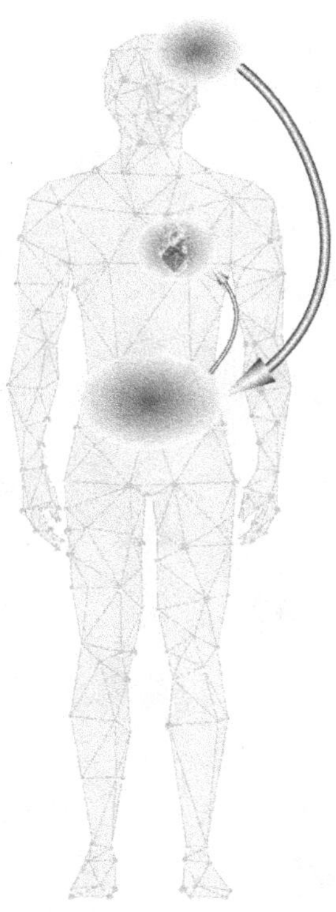

3rd Dimension of Physical Reality

Once created, thought acts as its own energetic signal which is then carried down to the etheric pathways of the lower chakra regions. There an intention, based on love or fear, is created and sent as yet another energetic signal to the heart chakra.

Left Brain Consciousness

Translation of Energy in Creating Your "Outer" Reality

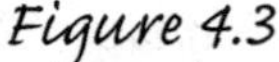

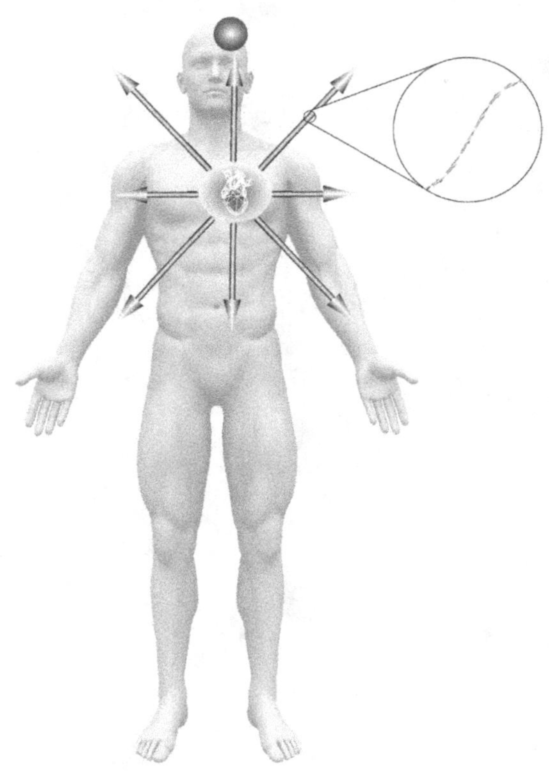

3rd Dimension of Physical Reality

Thought and emotion are translated by the heart chakra where it then emotes an electromagnetic field we know as feelings. Inwardly, these feelings are sent to the neural pathways of the body and the left brain hemisphere where the appropriate chemicals are released that define the genetic expression of each cell. Therefore, causing them to become the physical manifestation of our feelings. Outwardly, the same process occurs whereby feelings are used to define the genetic expression and physical reality of the universe. Since the process is controlled by the LBC, your physical reality becomes one of "reacting" to what is, rather than "creating" what can be.

In the new dream state, our mind is slowly exposed to the light of Truth. In doing so, we open ourselves to the Right Brain Consciousness which serves as the creative center of the mind. It is here where we begin to see ourselves as more than just the illusion of our physical bodies. As we ascend into the higher frequencies of this consciousness, a greater sense of separation from our egoic mind forms whereby we see ourselves for who we are – that is, Oneness with all that is divine energy.

It is as though you are in a movie and suddenly you realize that you have this extraordinary gift to step out of character and manipulate any scene in your life, in any conceivable way, at any time. You are no longer just the actor but also the writer, producer and director of your story. If this sounds familiar, it should, because this is exactly what happens in a lucid dream; thus, explaining why I had such dreams as a child. The dreams were meant to help me remember the experiential existence of the Right Brain Consciousness.

This is what is meant by being "in" this world but not "of" it. To know where you stand in relationship to the illusion that is being projected back to you is priceless. A remembrance of everything you once knew but had forgotten. The Right Brain Consciousness offers a portal by which to experience the deepest understanding that all is happening "by" you rather than "to" you. And, that all is happening in the present moment of the Now because now is all that exists in every dimension of creation.

The physical manifestations of the Right Brain Consciousness are more difficult to experience within the structural identity of our outer world. It is far more prevalent in our inner world where we can be, do or have anything at any time. However, the more you stay within this consciousness, the more you will see its presence in your outer reality. In time, you will begin to experience a higher occurrence of synchronicities that were not present before. Even more fascinating are the changes to your physical reality as people, places and things begin to characterize your conscious thoughts and emotions.

The mechanical aspects of the Right Brain Consciousness are not limited to our physical senses as it mainly relies on the meta-sensory capabilities of our beingness. Therefore, when energy is interpreted by the higher senses of our consciousness, a signal is sent to the etheric pathways of the mind which are completely independent of, but still located in and around, the right hemisphere of the brain.

Know that the processing capabilities of the Right Brain Consciousness are vastly superior since it interacts with the heart and Source chakras of our beingness. It is fully aware that energy is being interpreted from both the inward and outward experiences of the mind. As such, energy will either be rationalized into thought by the Left Brain Consciousness to manifest our outer reality or it will form the basis by which intentional desires are born that fuel the expansion of our inner world.

If the former, the process by which energy flows is similar to that of the Left Brain Consciousness reality. In the latter, the process becomes one where the meta-sensory energy flows directly to the Source chakras of Spirit. In time, the process becomes very deliberate in nature to create levels of gratitude and appreciation so great that all thought going forward inspires feelings of eternal peace, love, happiness and spiritual freedom *(see Figs. 4.4 through 4.6).*

Right Brain Consciousness

Translation of Energy in Creating Your "Inner & Outer" Realities

Figure 4.4

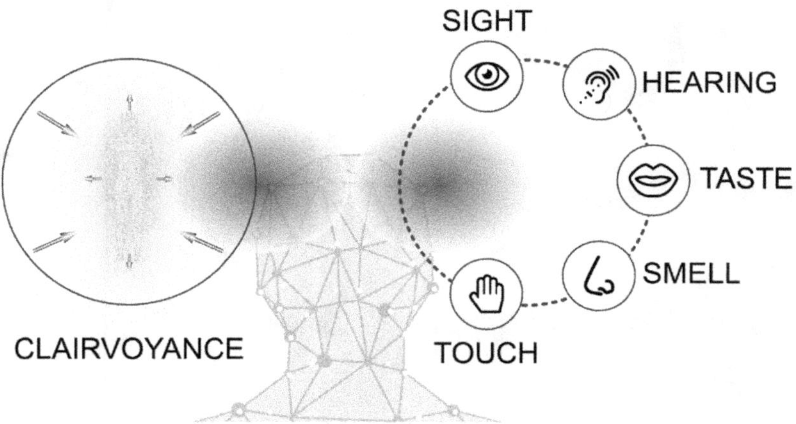

3rd to 4th Dimensions of Physical Reality

In the new dream state, an element of higher frequency is introduced that triggers our 6th sense(s) which are clairvoyant in nature. These frequencies are interpreted by the meta-sensory field of our beingness which surrounds our body. An energetic signal is then sent to the creative pathways of the Right Brain Consciousness (RBC). The signals are interpreted by the RBC as being part of your inner and outer experiences which are then reaffirmed by the creation of a thought.

Right Brain Consciousness

Translation of Energy in Creating Your "Inner & Outer" Realities

Figure 4.5

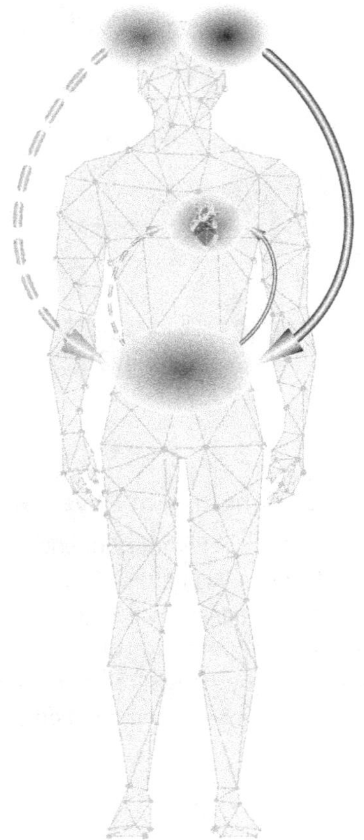

3rd to 4th Dimension of Physical Reality

As we ascend into the higher dimensions of the RBC, our mind is conflicted with dual interpretations of what we perceive to be reality. A part of us no longer associates itself with the egoic mind. Slowly we begin to realize that we might be "in" this world but not "of" it. This realization creates a split energy signal that is sent down to the etheric pathways of our lower chakra region. Intentions, based on love and/or fear are created and are sent as energetic signals to the heart chakra. The process of translating LBC thought and emotion into feelings remains the same. However, RBC thought and emotion are translated into desires which emote an

Right Brain Consciousness

Translation of Energy in Creating Your "Inner & Outer" Realities

Figure 4.5 (cont.)

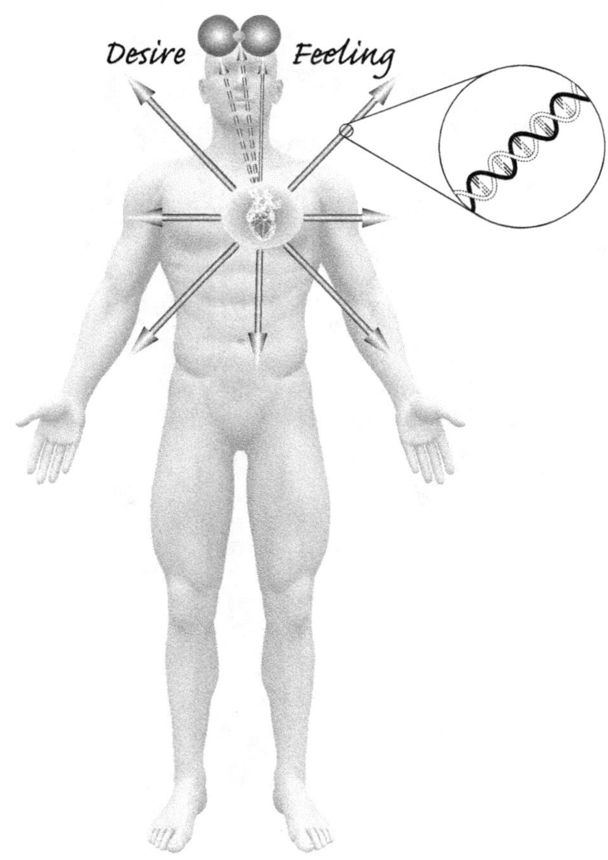

electromagnetic field to the central (i.e., pineal) and right brain hemispheres; thus, confirming and creating what can be in our inner reality. Notwithstanding, those same desires begin to bleed into our physical reality, creating an entirely new genetic expression (i.e., identity) relative to who we are and the universe within which we exist. (Note: Initially, RBC-related energy signals will be weaker which is illustrated by the dotted lines.)

Right Brain Consciousness

Translation of Energy in Creating Your "Inner & Outer" Realities

Figure 4.6

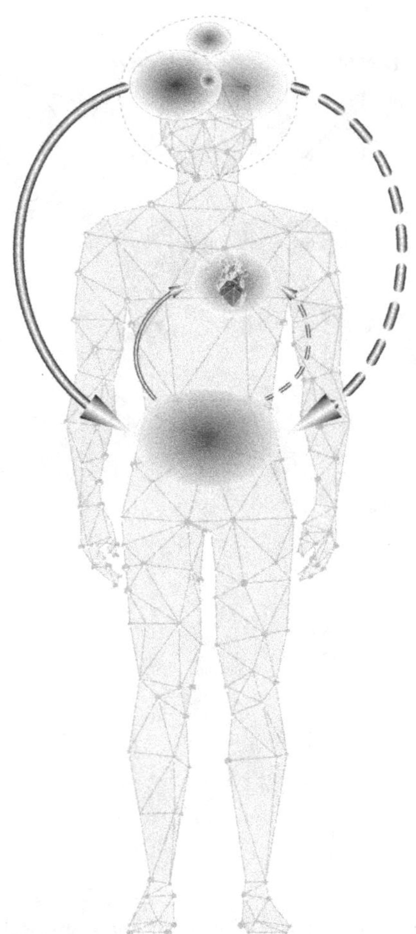

4th to 5th Dimension of Physical Reality

In time, our RBC becomes the dominant state of beingness which enables the translation of all outer and inner energy to flow to a more centralized location. Energy will either be "rationalized" or "experienced" into thought and emotion to manifest both your inner and outer realities. Since the RBC is now the dominant state, a conscious connection with the higher Self begins to form and intensify

Right Brain Consciousness

Translation of Energy in Creating Your "Inner & Outer" Realities

Figure 4.6 (cont.)

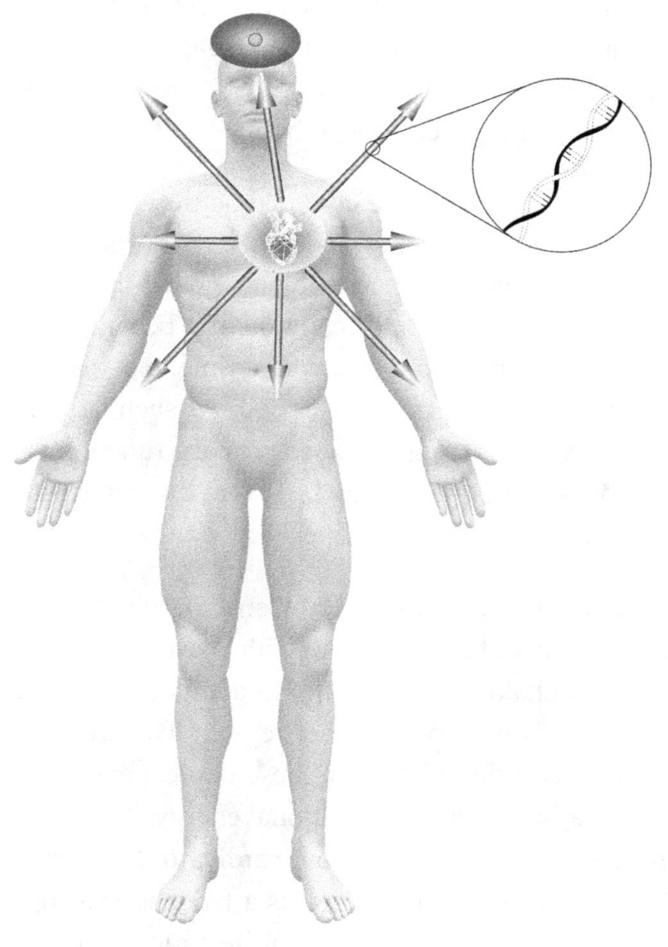

which inspires feelings and desires – now intertwined more tightly – of peace, love, happiness and spiritual freedom. Fear becomes virtually non-existent. The result being an electromagnetic field of connected beingness with all aspects of yourself and everything and everyone.

It is at this point that the God Consciousness is introduced. For the Right Brain Consciousness is simply here to facilitate the transition between the new dream state and the awakened state of our beingness. The God Consciousness is an evolution of the body, mind and soul where all three become One. It is the point in our evolution whereby we are completely reunited with our authentic Self; thus, no longer associated with any aspect of duality. We are free to dance with duality but are no longer controlled by it.

In the God Consciousness, we come home to who we really are as spiritual beings. Our beingness is centered on knowing ourselves as God as all three consciousness come together to form a supreme consciousness. Awareness and intentionality become the dominate forms of experiencing in a world where time and space take on an entirely new meaning, if they exist at all. As such, all energy flows in and out of this mind region whose primary function is to further the total expansion of our beingness. It is at this point that the walls between our inner and outer realities fade away.

The mechanical process of the God Consciousness is such that our bodies become very elastic in nature with an elongated skull to house the 7th and 8th chakras of the mind. In addition, there is a melding of all lower chakras into the heart region. Thought ascends into consciousness as it flows between these two expanded areas of the mind in a spiraling stream of intentional energy. That energy is then sent hurdling, both inwardly and outwardly, to all of creation in the form of blissful feelings. The result is a language so sophisticated, so profound in its intensity, that manifestation is instantaneous! *(see Figs. 4.7 through 4.9).*

A word of caution. Do not rationalize this state of beingness with the analytical mind, for it is ill equipped to fathom such possibilities. Though it exists all around us, the God Consciousness can only be experienced at the higher frequencies known as the 5th dimension and beyond. A state of dimensionality that is quickly approaching as our vibrational set point rises with the universal ascension into the new dream state.

God Consciousness

Translation of Energy in Creating a "Blended" Reality

Figure 4.7

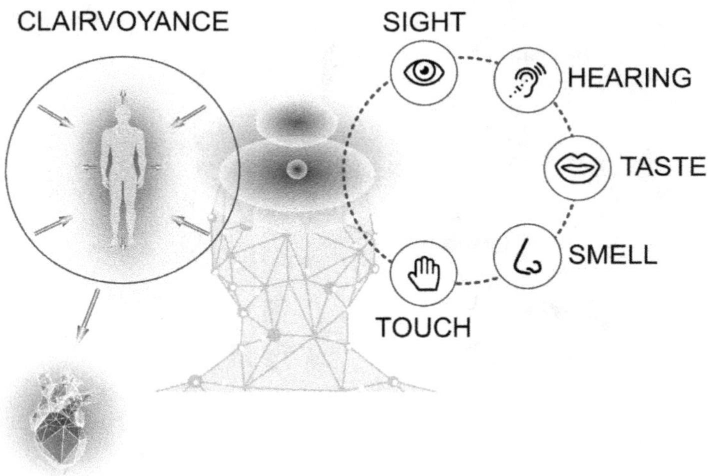

5th Dimension of Physical Reality

As frequencies rise, the transitional elements of the new dream state give way to an "awakened" state of beingness with the higher Self known as God Consciousness (GC). Our 6th senses are now communicating directly with the Source chakras of Spirit. Consciousness in the higher chakra region completes its melding process. In time, energetic signals from all senses are being interpreted from ONE expanded region. As your attention is drawn inward, the dominant signals will come from your inner reality. These signals will intensify and be interpreted as part of both your inner and outer experiences which is then reaffirmed by the creation of a thought.

God Consciousness

Translation of Energy in Creating a "Blended" Reality

Figure 4.8

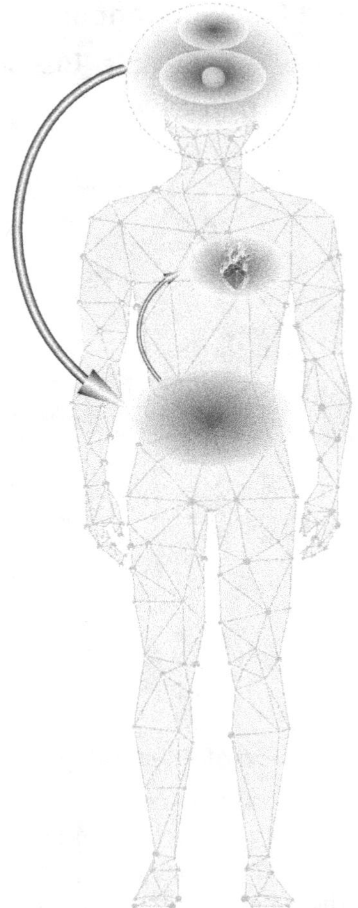

5th Dimension of Physical Reality

Coherency now exists among all regions of consciousness. Therefore, thought signals that are sent to the etheric pathways of the lower chakras are coherent in nature. Emotional signals, along with the desires and feelings that are created, are coherent as well. The result being, a melding of energetic frequencies that create a field of blissfulness. (Note: One of the physical manifestations of GC is an elongated skull region as illustrated by the dotted lines above the head. Therefore,

God Consciousness

Translation of Energy in Creating a "Blended" Reality

Figure 4.8 (cont.)

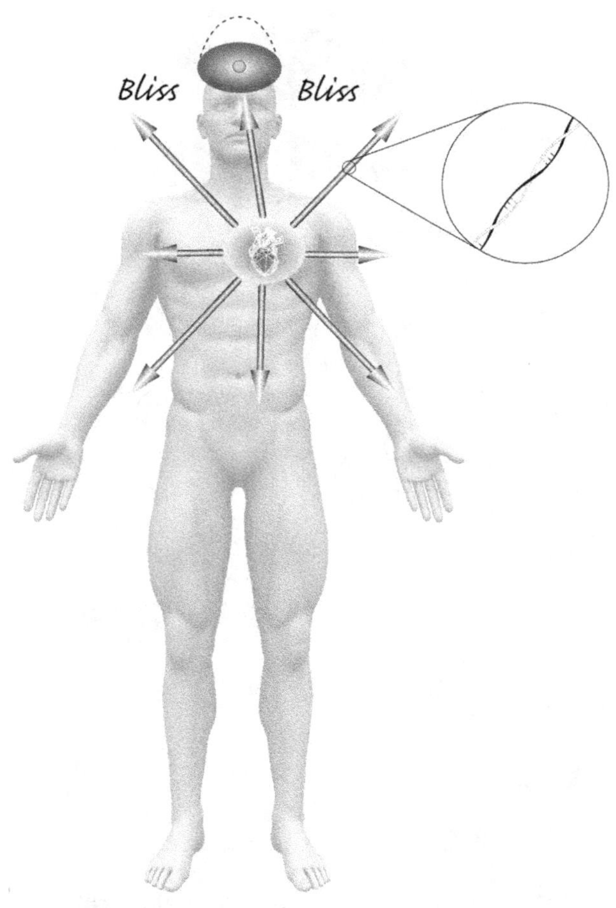

correlating with multiple descriptions of the "Star People" who lived among us in ancient times. Our relationship to these beings is discussed in more detail in Chapter Nine.)

God Consciousness

Translation of Energy in Creating a "Blended" Reality

Figure 4.9

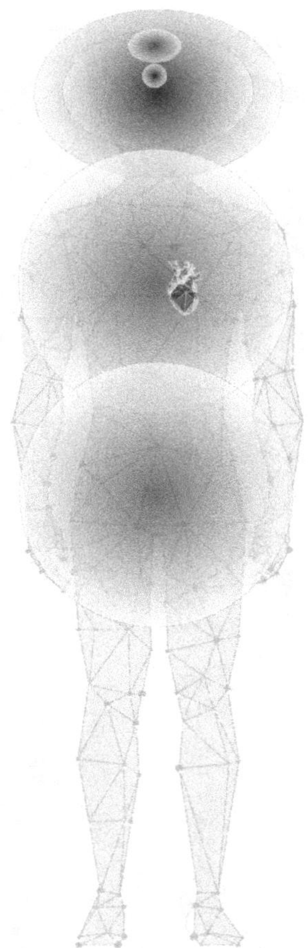

5th to 6th Dimension of Physical Reality

All regions of consciousness meld together as we near the higher frequencies of the 6th dimension. In time, we no longer need our physical bodies. Awareness and intentionality become the dominant forms of experiencing. We become an etheric essence of light dancing with duality. The melding of the inner and outer worlds will have come to a completion. What is left to experience is Heaven on Earth.

Nevertheless, many of you have or will experience an awakening whereby your natural tendency will be to rationalize everything within the context of your outer reality. What you will find is a world of extraordinary contradiction where sensibility is measured only by our willingness to conform to its insanity. For those brave enough to bite from the forbidden apple of the inner world, I beg you not to go in with the egoic mind.

Do not enter as the physical self who is armed with nothing more than the antiquated belief systems of the old dream state. If you do, you will certainly go mad as every fear you have ever known will be exposed and brought to the surface in a heightened state of panic. You will be blinded from the Truth, interpreting these fears as an affirmation of the pain and evil you see in your world rather than what it truly is – which is to say, the cleansing of your soul through the resurrection of the God Consciousness.

This is what was meant by our metaphorical banishment from the "Garden of Eden." This is the Truth that is spoken in so many of the ancient languages and traditions of our civilization. Many in plain view, begging to be reinterpreted so that we may see ourselves for who we really are. We have left so many clues, so many trails by which to experience our way back to our inner Self. If only we would allow ourselves to surrender to the inner Voice and experience it through a multitude of new lenses.

I say this to you because I have experienced this Truth first hand. I neglected all of its warnings and subjected myself to its painful lessons. I entered my inner world through the egoic mind and what I found was nothing less than horrifying. A world void of beauty, only because I was too naïve to think I was ready to receive its blessings. Ready to receive the Truth given my limited awareness of who I was as God. The hole I fell into was so ingested by fear that I vowed if I were to come out of this alive, I would share its secrets so that no one would ever have to experience a similar ordeal.

> *After the initial Downloads, my life took on more meaning as I could see an entirely new path being carved out for me. A path I was determined to take with great conviction. Though I was eternally grateful for the peace Caleb had brought to my life, it never occurred to me to align myself with its wisdom before embarking on my inner quest. Instead, I chose to interpret the Downloads within the limited construct of my egoic mind.*
>
> *It wasn't long before my inner quest took on an entirely new meaning. My mind became obsessed in manipulating these Truths to justify their sensibility relative to the madness of my outer reality. Hoping that in doing so, it would inspire something out there to change in some dramatic fashion. Never thinking that all I needed was to simply "be still and know." To know that the only change that mattered was the one within me. In doing so, my outer world would change instantaneously.*
>
> *In hindsight, Caleb's teachings were simply too overwhelming for me at the time. I was barely managing to keep up with life, much less try to experience it from an entirely new perspective. The process of maintaining the status quo required so little mind muscle that by default, it became the obvious way by which to live. I had become so entrenched in the dream state that anything challenging it was simply unacceptable. As a result, I missed out on a*

wonderful opportunity to experience the enjoyment of "coming out" earlier in my life.

I also made too many flawed assumptions relative to my physical reality and my purpose in it. For instance, rather than using this new consciousness to ascend into a higher reality, I chose to distort its Truths to justify the epic battle in my mind between good and evil. Rather than dance with duality, I chose to vilify it. "And for what purpose?" you will ask. That's simple – to give my life the meaning it never had within the illusion of my physical reality. Looking back, I am appalled at how badly I misinterpreted what Caleb had spent a lifetime preparing me to receive.

Without notice to my fragile ego, I embarked on an inner quest so devoid of love, so engrossed in fear, that within six months of experiencing my initial Downloads, I found myself asleep again. Living a nightmare from which I could not escape. Worse yet, I would bring others into my distorted reality not realizing how vulnerable they too were to their own fears. A frantic sense of emptiness engulfed my world leaving me gasping for life. I knew things were spiraling out of control, but lacked the wherewithal to understand why or how to get out.

As fate would have it, one morning I woke up to a familiar sound in my mind. One I hadn't heard in months. It was a gentle sound that seemed to be whispering my name as if to softly awaken me from my slumber. Though its essence appeared rather odd to me, I knew it was Caleb. "I missed you," I whispered quietly as if somehow I would wake up the house with the sound of my thoughts. Though I heard nothing, vibrationally I could sense that Caleb's visit had little to do with saving me from my self-inflicted wounds.

"You have misunderstood what you were shown," Caleb proceeded. "You are not ready. You must build your armor and learn to use it wisely, for your path will be difficult and you will be challenged by many along the way. It will be five years before the door opens again, but we assure you it will. At which time, you will experience a prolonged awakening as you gradually get accustomed to the Truth. Then and only then will your light shine for others to see. For now, you are not ready!" And just like that my mind went silent.

What would ensue would be a period of darkness so deep that no light could penetrate through it. I was left alone to pick up the pieces of my life. Oblivious to what laid ahead in the troubling spaces of my inner world. If only I had listened I would have known that my inner world held the key by which to escape from the outer hell I had created. Instead, I toiled in the deepest depths of depression for years, wondering if I would ever hear from Caleb again.

I share this story not to frighten you, but rather to illustrate a point. A point worth repeating as often as needed, for its significance has been misinterpreted many times over the ages. That is to say, there will come a time when you will be reunited with your inner Voice. A Voice that you have known for many lifetimes. One that knows you better than you know yourself and who is eager for you to remember the same. That Voice will come and it will show you the way. And when it does, you need not be afraid. Let it show you the dream state that you and only you have created, for it will also show you the path by which to escape. I know this is inconceivable to the analytical mind, but I promise that when the time comes you will know what to do.

To enter into your inner reality will require you to do so void of your physical identity. In the metaphysical world, you are faceless and that is how you must enter. You must be pure consciousness and though you believe you are not, you most definitely are! For one does not have to leave this earthly existence through death to experience oneself as pure consciousness. You can access this state of beingness at any time, for the stage has been set for us to do so as we ascend into the higher frequencies of the new dream state.

But how does one come to this point? How does one begin to fathom themselves as God experiencing itself through the duality of a human existence? Much less, understand the esoteric nature of this discussion to enter into God Consciousness long enough to stay awake. Where does one begin in our spiritual quest to reunite ourselves with our inner Voice? The one Voice who stands ready to guide us through the unchartered waters of our inner world. To help us manifest every desire we have come to realize.

The answers lie within the Attributes of your etheric armor. Separately, they possess the power by which to experience any facet of your divinity. Together, they produce an energy so great that the slightest fluctuation to its collective frequency would cause a ripple-effect throughout the universe.

So magical are they, that when used in accordance with the Laws of the Universe, they can change your physical reality in a blink of an eye. So profound is the experience that you will be taken to the deepest regions of your inner world, where your authentic Self awaits.

A state of beingness so blissful that its sheer presence will mark the arrival of what has been foretold over many millennia as the coming of Heaven on Earth!

Chapter Five

The Attributes

It would be five years before I would learn of the Attributes that make up my spiritual armor. It would be another two years before I would come to appreciate the language it would allow me to speak. A language that would enable me to give new meaning to feelings I knew merely on a superficial level. Feelings from the heart that only the Universe could understand. A language of frequency we can neither see nor hear, but I assure you it exists. As with any language, it takes a considerable amount of time and practice before one is able to articulate thoughts and emotions in any coherent manner. It also takes focus and determination, but I promise that if you were to apply these Attributes to your life, the world that would await you would be unlike any other.

In the original dream state, you are kept clueless as to the power of your Attributes. Your mind is held captive to what "is" rather than what "can be" in your life. Always experiencing itself as an endless loop of redundancy. Reacting to a world in a tireless game of *Cause and Effect,* never considering the possibility that YOU are responsible for causing the effect! And so, day in and day out, you plug away at life unaware of the power you possess to drastically change it. To reawaken a higher state of consciousness by simply using the Attributes of your mind.

Yet, through the evolution of this outer reality we are entering a period that marks the physical manifestation of the new dream state. A time of global awakening where the gateway to the inner world is accessible to all who are willing to trust their inner Voice. No longer will we be isolated from the clues we have left behind. Clues intended to help us remember – to help us wake up!

Many will fight to stay asleep. Choosing to use their Attributes to perform the mindless task of creating a rudimentary language designed to reinforce the primitive belief systems within which they have been operating since the beginning of time. Constructs that would have us believe that everything, including God, exists somewhere *out there* for us to please and respond to as a puppet would to a puppeteer. Unable or unwilling to break the habitual patterns that have kept us from realizing our true Self.

The Attributes I speak of many of you know all too well. For some, I know it will be tempting to discard their importance. I urge you not to fall victim to your skepticism, for it will be one of your greatest regrets going forward. I chose to discard their importance through the darkest years of my life. A period I painfully refer to as the "Lost Years." These were extraordinary years full of trials and tribulations that preceded my second awakening. An awakening that would come one evening in October on my 51st birthday.

> *It had been five years since I last spoke to Caleb. My life had become an emotional and spiritual disaster. I was lost in a physical world I had nothing in common with other than my family who embodied the remaining vestiges of sanity I held firmly in my*

world. I had come so close to experiencing everything I had wished for spiritually in my life only to have it ripped away by none other than yours truly. Banished to a world where my only companions were the fears I had conjured up from my past.

Angry and confused, I fell back into my old habits and accepted the archaic interpretation that I had somehow offended God and was being punished for my sins. My rational mind was no match for the hell I was creating in the dream state. No longer was I just a prisoner to the social construct, for I had taken on the unwanted role of judge, jury and executioner of my life.

It wasn't long before I was joined by yet another companion whose control over me was unlike anything I had ever encountered. I had fallen into a deep state of depression where I walked a non-existent life, void of any meaningful light to feed my starving soul. A mental state of purgatory where one experiences their physicality through a hazy mist that never lifts.

I bought into the lies that my ego had gotten the best of me. That I had fallen prey to my weakness for self-righteousness. I hated myself for having given into the ridiculous notion that I was God. How could I have been so blinded by my arrogance to believe that I could be more than just some submissive creature in this play of life? For years, I would carry this burden of shame, haunted by the guilt of disobedience bestowed upon me by the social conditioning of my past.

Day after day, I would awaken to a suffocating feeling of despair. An anxiety so unbearable that it would jolt me into submission and leave me begging to be put out of my misery. I wandered through life as a mere shell of my physical existence. I was afraid to share my ordeal with anyone, much less my family. I was embarrassed at what I had done with my life and how I had put my family at risk. A sense of inadequacy filled my heart as I could not bear to think that I had wasted my life chasing a dream that never existed other than in my delusional state of mind.

Slowly, I put the pieces of my life together again. I even began a nightly ritual of having a conversation with God; albeit, a one-sided conversation with a being that was once again somewhere "out there." It felt rather superficial at times, but I was ecstatic to have some semblance of my life back. No matter what life would throw at me, I was prepared to play by its rules and accept the consequences as further retribution for my crimes.

In time, Caleb's armor became nothing more than a horrible metaphor for the egoic mindset I chose to embrace. For better or for worse, I was determined to treat life in the same manner that I felt it was treating me – with anger and disregard for others. I was prepared to use my insecurities as weapons to justify my behavior. Looking back, the only victims in this horrible tragedy were my loved ones. For these may have been the Lost Years, but to my family they would come to be known as the "Angry Years."

And so it went on until the eve of my 51st birthday when I received a rather unassuming text from Sharlene with a video attached to it. The video was of a woman who had been diagnosed with cancer but whose life had been saved through a procedure known as energy healing. As I watched, I could not help but feel that I was somehow receiving a message of healing from somewhere deep within.

The message had a sense of urgency that made me listen more deeply to the words being said in the video. It was as if a pattern was emerging in my mind with certain words being highlighted to indicate their significance. And though their relevance to me was not immediate, I could sense that they were forming a message my heart could understand.

Within minutes, wave after wave of messages were crashing onto the unsuspecting shores of my mind in places I had forbidden myself to re-enter. A sense of disbelief came over me as I was once again receiving Downloads. I didn't know exactly what I had done to trigger this event, but I knew I didn't want it to end. I closed my eyes and prayed silently that the curse I had been living with all these years had somehow been lifted and that the Downloads were here to rescue me from my spiritual hell.

Though they would last only a few minutes, it was long enough for me to remember what it felt like to be awakened. To appreciate the moment as if it were the only gift that mattered. I hung on to each moment thereafter, not knowing or caring if I would remember any of it the next day. All I wanted was to savor every bit of its beauty as if it were my last.

The next day, though I would awaken to the familiar feelings of my past, I could sense that my life had changed. I knew something remarkable had happened and though brief, I knew the Downloads were Caleb's doing. I sensed it was their way of assuring me that the end was near. That there was reason to be hopeful and that I had not been forgotten. Regrettably, by nightfall I had lost the battle to remember yet again.

That evening, as I toiled over some meaningless paperwork, I could feel hope slipping away into the murky waters of forgetfulness. I was immersed in numbers and totally oblivious to the preparations that had begun around me to celebrate my birthday. I was sitting at the dining room table when suddenly I felt a rather familiar sense of separation in my mind. As in my lucid dreams, I felt I was consciously pulling away from my conditioned self, as if there were two of us now sharing the same body.

"I'm not letting go," I thought to myself as I knew a door had opened in my mind that could lead me back to freedom. Just then a voice whispered the words my heart had waited to hear all these years, "You are home now. We have been here waiting for you." My eyes swelled up with tears as I heard Caleb's unmistakable voice once again.

The haze that had followed me all these years began to lift and I could see and hear the joyous sounds of my family. My heart could breathe again as it took

> *in all the love that was being directed my way. I sat there in silence as wave after wave of gratitude and appreciation filled my consciousness. I was home again, in more ways than one. Though I wasn't quite sure how I did it, I found my way back to me – the authentic me I knew as God. A path of remembrance that has remained open to me to this day.*

Unbeknownst to me, Caleb was in constant communication throughout my Lost Years. Sending signs or clues to help me through life no matter how faint or subtle they may have appeared. It wasn't Caleb who tried severing the connection – it was me. I chose not to tune into their frequency. It was my choice to view the world through a set of lenses that prevented me from seeing that the only one stopping me from being me was me!

Since I knew nothing of my Attributes, I foolishly rejected their significance whenever Caleb presented them in my life. They were simply too simple and too pure to be relevant in this world. Unfortunately, they were relegated to a place so abstract, so obsolete, that I rarely gave any thought to them. To me, they were mere child's play in a world that demanded an "Eat or be Eaten" mentality. Looking back, I cannot believe how foolish I was to have discarded their importance.

Going forward, I urge you not to make the same mistake. That you refrain from relying on your analytical mind in making sense of what is being revealed. Instead, let what needs to flow into your analytical mind flow while allowing the rest to cascade through your experiential mind. Listen with your heart and let your intuition guide you to where you need to be. To that end, I will explain the Attributes not as concepts, but rather as mystical elements of your spiritual mind.

Know that each Attribute creates an energy signature capable of transcending any reality at any time. I have alluded to these frequencies before, but I want to take a moment to share their importance going forward. You see, every energy that exists in the physical and metaphysical contains its own unique signature. It is as unique to that energy as the name that was given to you at birth. If you are to navigate your way back home, you will need to understand how to use your Attributes to create the language whose energy signature will guide you to your destination.

I spent my entire life downplaying my Attributes. In fact, I did everything I could to avoid them. Today, they are as important to me as breathing. I owe my life to them. It is with the greatest respect that I will share with you their secrets, if only at a cursory level. For you see, there is still so much I need to share. Therefore, I will have to elaborate more on these another time. For now, I will provide you with what is needed to help you wake up from the dream state.

Imagination

In the original dream state, I was led to believe that to imagine was an exercise in futility. I have since learned that nothing could be further from the Truth. In awakening to the new dream state, I have come to realize that everything we do as spiritual beings revolves around our imagination. That any form of the dream state could not have existed without our desire to imagine it. Nevertheless, as a child I was taught by those I admired to abandon my imagination for the practical uses of my analytical mind. I had no reason to question them, for these people loved me and wanted only the best for me. Little did I know that their dreams had been shattered years before by those they had revered, or worse yet, by those they had come to fear.

In the new dream state, I came to realize that every thought I had or image I had perceived was merely my imagination in action. Likewise, every physical experience was nothing more than the manifestation of my imagination reflecting itself in a lower frequency of energy. As Caleb once said to me, "In the world of consciousness, imagination inspires everything!" As for the remaining Attributes, their contributions would be significant as well. For if imagination was the magic, then they were the "elixir." The secret sauce, if you will, that could bring the magic to life.

"So if everything is a product of my imagination, why can't I make my dreams come true?" you will ask. Like in *The Sorcerer's Apprentice,* you must learn how to use your Attributes to create and direct your imagination. In the original dream state, we are led to believe that the only form of imagination allowed is the one that supports the action-oriented goals of both your ego and social constructs. Constructs that do not exist other than, you guessed it, in your imagination. Nevertheless, we have become great masters at taking direction from constructs that don't even exist. Limiting our imagination to those things that matter least to us.

I need you to stop and absorb what was just said, for I tell you now that you are being given a sign so blatant that dismissing it would be a travesty. That is, everything you believe to be real does not exist unless you imagine it to exist. To believe otherwise is to believe in a lie that you and only you can break out of because you are the one creating the lie. I don't blame you if this is twisting your mind in ways you cannot accept or comprehend, but at a much deeper level I know it makes sense for it is a Truth you came here to remember.

The most beloved teachers and the most renowned minds in history have known the Truth behind the power of imagination. Even some of the most respected leaders in technology today have, or are speaking to, the power of imagination as not just some abstract concept to consider, but rather the magic behind the greatest innovations of our time. Innovations that many of these great thinkers will tell you came from some divine source of inspiration. And yet, we sit there and dismiss this Truth time and time again. Ignoring one of the most powerful Attributes we have gifted ourselves in the name of complacency or fear of the unknown.

It goes without saying that without imagination, reality as we know it would cease to exist – immediately! So then, what is it that holds you back from creating the world you desire versus simply reinforcing the one you inherited? The answer, lies in part, within the Attribute we know of as faith. An Attribute which has been grossly misunderstood to keep us oblivious to its power and its ability to bring our imagination to life.

Faith

In the original dream state, we are led to believe that faith is entirely dependent on rational thinking. That it is intertwined with the physical senses, for if we can hear, see, taste, smell or touch our reality, it must be real, and therefore our faith cannot be questioned.

We often throw faith around with other terms such as hope, think, feel or belief. Giving little or no thought as to what any of them truly mean. But as I awoke to the new dream state, I was reminded that faith, in its purest sense, was severely limited within the borders of my physical reality.

It was there that I was shown a new way to view faith within the context of its metaphysical power to create worlds. I use the term "metaphysics" because it often implies a more contemporary view of mysticism. Notwithstanding, it is time to let go of this archaic notion that mysticism is somehow equated to the occult, for in its purest, most authentic sense, it is not. In the new dream state, I came to know that many of our modern spiritual practices, including some of our greatest religions, came from such origins. Origins that have always been faithful to the universal Oneness of Love.

"So how does faith play into imagination?" you will ask. First, you must understand that faith can take on many forms depending on the frequency within which it is being used. This is absolutely critical in understanding why, in many instances, faith is unable to manifest your desires. Secondly, as powerful as faith may seem it is still only one Attribute. Therefore, to achieve your desires you must learn to use faith in combination with some or all of your Attributes. I will illustrate this point in the next chapter. For now, I will focus on the first point.

Imagine faith as a spectrum of energy. On the left side of the spectrum you will find the most analytical form of faith known as thinking. This is the realm within which the rational mind exists and tries to express itself as beingness. In the original dream state, I was led to believe that thinking was everything. I marveled at how it defined western civilization and how its control over our world seemed to be spreading every day. In the new dream state, I came to view thinking as the "weakest" link in my chain of faith. I was shown how thinking functioned at the lowest levels of vibration and how it created from a place of what "is" rather than what "can be." Too often reinforcing a reality based on lack, rather than the limitless possibilities that exist in the Now.

Looking back, I cannot tell you how many times I used the words, "I 'think' I can," when confronted with a challenge. This was my analytical mind rationalizing an event in the only language I knew how to speak. A language that clung to the past in determining the probability of whatever outcome I was contemplating in the present.

This was the world of my Left Brain Consciousness. The world of, "I think therefore I am." Despite the many defining moments in my life, I chose to remain in the lowest frequency of thinking, rarely aspiring beyond wanting or hoping. All of which were dependent on external factors that were beyond my control.

Growing up, I used these lower frequencies to limit my imagination to those things I felt worthy of achieving within the confines of my social construct. I misunderstood the message of my spiritual teachers that tried to bring higher forms of faith to humanity. A message that was meant to point me in a different direction. To show me that faith had nothing to do with thinking, wanting or hoping. Rather, that its power existed in my ability to go beyond thought to a state of beingness where I could be that which I desired. I cannot stress the enormity of this message, for it makes up the basis by which miracles exist in our world.

Some of you will be surprised to know that the deepest form of faith is not in the act of believing. Believing serves merely to bridge our faith from the Left Brain Consciousness to the Right Brain Consciousness. Consequently, it is still vulnerable to the analytical mind which is immersed in the illusion of what lies *out there*. Despite the power of our beliefs, there is still this sense that we are battling the controls of our external world. That beliefs are simply thoughts that can be contained by using the rules of our physical reality.

Despite their limitations, beliefs did help me to use my imagination to further my desires. In the new dream state, I was shown how beliefs were born from the collaborative process between the mind, heart and soul which were designed to supersede all dream states. I began to realize that there was something more to me than what I would see in my reflection. That something deep within me was calling me to greatness. To embrace the power of my imagination in my quest to align my physical self with my authentic Self.

The act of believing forced me to dig deeper into the world of my feelings. To find those feelings that could fuel my passion and drive my determination. These feelings would introduce me to the language of the heart which is the only language spoken by the Universe. A language that vibrates at a much higher frequency than our physical reality. And since all matter is simply energy vibrating at a lower state of frequency, the act of believing offered me a glimpse of what was possible, not just in my mind, but in the physical world that was yet to come.

In the new dream state, many of you have or will soon experience a transition from believing to "knowing" your beingness. This will be your tipping point where you will no longer accept the limited interpretation of who you are. It is here where you will begin to sense your true identity as Oneness with all. And in knowing this Truth, you will be required to fully understand how to use your faith. Understand that the act of knowing is meant to refer to a higher state of consciousness that transcends all doubt. As such, you will come to know the world of what "can be" rather than what "is."

But to "know" this is not enough to fully awaken. You must go beyond knowing to a place of "understanding," whereby you become that which you have faith in. To take a leap so enormous that you will awaken the child within you to imagine in ways you have forgotten. It is here where you will use your imagination in the manner that it was meant to be used. That is, to remember and experience yourself as God in every imaginable way possible!

Awareness

"But I don't have that kind of faith," many of you will say. "I wouldn't know how to access it even if I wanted to." I tell you now that all of you have this faith because you are using it every day to create the reality you have come to know through your five senses. Right now there is a part of you, hidden deep within your Left Brain Consciousness, which is absolutely aware of every aspect of your environment. Continuously communicating with the Universe to manifest any reality you deem to be real, over and over again. Do you know what kind of faith is required to continuously create the world you are experiencing?

The piece that is missing is your "inner" awareness that what you are intuitively sensing or creating through your imagination is as real, if not more so, than your physical world. "So what is awareness?" you will ask. Simply put, awareness is your ability to acknowledge your existence outside of this physical world. To know that you are more than what you see in your reflection. But to know this concept is not enough – it must be "felt." Therefore, you must first know how to access it through the stillness that exists in your inner world.

"But how do I get there?" you will ask. "My mind is too chaotic to allow for such stillness to exist!" I assure you that no mind can exist without stillness. In fact, nothing can exist without stillness. For it is at the center of all creation. Admittedly, I struggled mightily with this point. For me, my mind had become too twisted, too distorted to allow for such beauty to exist. That is of course until Caleb came to my rescue and showed me the way.

> *One morning as I was waking up, I heard Caleb's voice in the distance. "Look up," Caleb said as I could feel the gentle tug of a hand. "Look at where we are. Do you recognize it?" Though my eyes were closed,*

an image began to appear. "Yes, I know this place. I've been here many, many times before. I know it like the back of my hand. It's my home!" I cried, as I could barely contain my excitement. "This is my beautiful meadow that I have dreamt about since I was a child."

I paused for a moment as I took in the splendor of my world. As I looked around, I could feel my heart bursting with joy. "How did I get here?" I asked, in total bewilderment. "This feels too good to be a dream." I could feel my resistance mounting as though there was something telling me that such beauty could not exist in any world, much less mine. That this meadow was only a figment of my imagination, and therefore undeserving of my time and attention. Besides, what good would it do to surrender myself to its beauty if I couldn't stay to appreciate it?

"This is your world," Caleb said confidently, as if they knew exactly what I was thinking. "This is not somewhere you have to go. It is where you have always been and where you will always find your inner Self. For you have never left your home which is why it was so easy for you to find it. Everything that is you is represented here. Everyone and everything that matters to you is here and will always be here. All you have to do is 'be still and know.' Let go of the resistance and surrender yourself to the beauty of your inner world."

That morning, Caleb opened my eyes to a world that existed beyond my physical senses. A world that was more real to me than anything my analytical mind could conceive. That I didn't have to go looking for this thing called the stillness because I am and will always be the stillness. For you cannot leave that which you are in essence. All you have to do is open the doors to your imagination and remember the place you call "home" deep within. I assure you it is there and it will be as vivid to you as anything in the world of your physical senses.

Anchor yourself to your awareness and you will soon feel the serenity within the silence of your inner world. Feel as it penetrates the deepest regions of your beingness. Let go of the resistance and it will happen quickly. Stay in this state of beingness as long as you can. And when you are ready, and only when you are ready, open your eyes and see how the chaos in your life has diminished, if not completely disappeared.

It is here that you will find your faith. A faith that carries no doubt, no insecurities, no fears of any kind. To reinforce that faith, you need only to turn your awareness inward to the only world that matters. In doing so, you will allow your imagination to run freely between both worlds. Do this as often as you need to, for this is your doorway to your Right Brain Consciousness. A state of awareness that knows no limit to what you are capable of achieving.

Though this may sound esoteric I assure you it is not. For I have already explained that we are constantly creating our reality based on the illusion that something exists *out there*. We have become so good at reinforcing this awareness that we have forgotten that what exists *out there* must first begin in the consciousness of our mind. I ask you then, what will you be capable of when you drop all resistance to this Truth? Imagine, if you can, the incredible feats humanity will accomplish when it does the same!

Intention

Have you ever wondered why so many efforts have failed despite being well intentioned? It is because most originate from a place of fear rather than love. I know this seems a bit irrational but allow me to explain. Intention is the ability to generate thought from a place of "having," which in turn is born from one of two emotions – love or fear.

Remember there is only one true emotion and that is love, but in the world of duality we must contend with the illusion of fear to fully appreciate love through contrast. Therefore, when we place our attention on what we do not want or have, which is what most of our efforts do, we give birth to fear. That is, the fear of lack. And since our attention is on the lack that inspired the effort, the Universe has no choice but to continue reciprocating that lack.

Looking back, I am appalled at how I chose to view my life. I wanted peace but I surrendered to my madness. I wanted happiness but could not see beyond my despair. I wanted love but believed I wasn't worthy of it. My life had become this huge obsession over wanting and needing which only added to my misunderstanding of duality. It wasn't until much later that I came to realize the true purpose of duality. That duality wasn't here to torture me relative to what I did not have, but rather it was here to remind me that I already had it! I simply needed to wake up and remember.

Have you ever noticed how some movements have been so successful using tactics that appeared to be counter-intuitive? The best example would be the many peace movements that have averted war, time and time again. In those instances, the attention was not on the oppression but rather on the presence of peace. Therefore, the intention itself came from a place of peace. In other words, where we place our attention is where we place our intention. If we are peace and want more of it, the Universe will make it happen. Peace is harmonious with love and love will always conquer fear. It is the Law of the Universe.

Remember you are pure love regardless of what you have been taught to believe. As such, you came here to experience the splendor of this Truth through contrast. Let that contrast be your reminder of your true intention and give that your focus. Nurture your desires with an unshakeable faith that what you desire has already happened, and I tell you now it will come to pass. For if you have mastered the creation of a fear-based reality, I assure you that you will do that and much more when you learn to create from a place of loving intention.

Compassion

But the quest does not end at intention, for you must allow yourself to experience the Attribute of compassion if you are to see the beauty in yourself and the world around you. I will warn you now that this is not an easy task. You will be challenged every step of the way to examine your convictions relative to how you view yourself and humanity as a whole. It is here where you will come face-to-face with the most discriminating of all behaviors – the pathological urge to judge.

Though it is generally accepted that such behavior is unbecoming, its repercussions go way beyond the issues of morality. As I have stated, the outer world is merely a reflection of your inner reality. It is an expression of how you view yourself in the dream state. Therefore, when you pass judgement on others you are doing so to some facet of yourself. Can you see how such behavior can create an endless cycle of fear within you if that judgement is aimed at blaming someone or something *out there* for your lot in life? Look closely and you will see the twisted irony in such conduct. A brilliant trap to keep you stuck in the dream state.

Compassion is about leaving judgement at the door. Not just judgment of others, but more importantly, judgement in yourself. If you cannot see the beauty or light within you, I assure you that the Universe will replicate that reality in the people or circumstances of your outer world. This includes the most unassuming and yet crippling of all judgments – that is, our propensity to "doubt" ourselves! But you do not have to take my word on this, for there is a growing amount of science and personal awareness that is now revealing this Truth.

Use compassion, not just to sympathize with others, but to recognize the beauty in everything through the eyes of empathy, despite how undesirable it may seem on the surface. More importantly, use compassion to recognize the same in yourself. Though there are many themes that run through my life, none seem to be more blatant then my propensity to judge every facet of myself. I cannot tell you how difficult it once was to look at myself in the mirror, much less with genuine compassion. To stare right through my reflection and see me for the light that I am.

At first, it was rather awkward to do so, if not painful. To stare at myself with love rather than fear was something I had never been taught to do. To tell myself over and over again that "no one was more worthy of compassion than me" was at times, surreal to say the least. In time, however, the world around me began to change, and with it went the illusion of my original dream state. As with intention, I would learn to bypass the trappings of the egoic mind and use compassion to go directly into the stillness of my silence.

As you venture inward, remember that compassion is there to remind you that everything is pure, loving energy. That this energy has transformed itself in this physical reality to reflect the manner in which you see yourself. Even the most negative energies disguised as a person, place or thing are as pure in their essence as any thought, feeling or emotion. Challenge yourself to remember this Truth. For if you do, you will come to experience your authentic Self in everything that is your physical reality. In other words, there will be no beginning nor end to you, just Oneness with all.

Gratitude & Appreciation

I have spent most of my life giving little thought to the acts of gratitude or appreciation. That is of course, until faced with some catastrophic event that would leave me grasping for any form of relief or rescue I could find. Even then, I could feel the emptiness in my heart as I reached for shallow words of thankfulness simply out of fear. Simply to stay afloat in a world that was consuming me alive. And yet, I could sense that in the midst of my plight, I was analyzing my behavior as if I were trying to remind myself of something greater.

Though I knew my words were insincere at the time, there was something beneath it all that my actions were provoking. As with compassion, there was this intrinsic sense that if I could somehow feel gratitude and appreciation in the worst of times, I could begin to see these qualities in everything that was transpiring in all facets of my life. Once again, it was the act of "feeling" these specific Attributes that would enable me to go deeper into my inner world in search of my authentic Self.

In time, I also came to realize that gratitude was a state of mind that supported the reality I was placing my attention on. That it served to create a focus so prevailing that my analytical mind was unable to differentiate between what I perceived to be real and what I was imagining to be real. And since my analytical mind was tasked with the responsibility of manifesting what I placed my attention on, the ability to express gratitude for what was yet to be, would create an unstoppable force of consciousness through my imagination.

Another key to remember is that gratitude is about giving thanks for what "is" as much as it is about what "will be" in your reality. For it is impossible to build a bridge between what is and what has yet to become if the foundation of one is not similar to the other. This is the Law of Resonance which states that two like energies are drawn to each other if they are both emitting the same frequency. In simple terms, like attracts like. Therefore, if you are to find your higher Self you must imagine that you already are your higher Self and be grateful for it.

As difficult as it may seem, give thanks for everything in your life. Show the constructs of your mind that you are blessed for the gifts that you have been given. That they serve a purpose in helping you to remember who you are, which in actuality, they do. Use gratitude to build the bridge between who you have become and who you know yourself to be as God. If you do, I promise that you will begin to create a momentum of positivity so strong that the Universe will have no choice but to recognize your divinity as your dominant frequency. And when that happens, be assured that it will be reflected in the manifestations of your outer world.

Appreciation is simply a deeper awareness of gratitude. It requires you to understand and ultimately feel the infiniteness of each moment. To feel that you are much more than who you know yourself to be in physicality. A recognition that you are perfection. That your physical reality is a game to enjoy rather than fear. That it serves to challenge you with clues and riddles as to your true identity. It is a profound awareness that you are experiencing the most magnificent creation of self-expression imaginable. That nothing in your physical reality would exist if it were not for you.

"But my life is nothing but pain," you will say. "How can I appreciate a life that has caused me to feel so worthless, so confused, so lost?"

Avoid the temptation of listening to your egoic mind as it will try to lure you back into the madness of your outer reality. Appreciate the serenity as you let your imagination roam freely in the world of higher Consciousness. It is that serenity that will engulf the chaotic world of your analytical mind so that you may re-enter your physical reality as your true Self. A state of beingness where you can observe and appreciate the illusory world of the dream state while you play with its duality.

"This is all a bunch of philosophical bullshit," you will say. I tell you now that it is not. The days of duality as a means by which to experience yourself as contrast are coming to an end. That if you were to appreciate each moment as a new expression of yourself, you would come to know a greater Truth that governs your outer reality. That is, each moment is free from any condition you call your past. Free from the illusion you call your future. Free to become its own independent reality. This is what you came here to know in order to liberate yourself from the dream state. Appreciate that Truth and it will set you free.

Affirmation

As a child, I was exposed to a barrage of negative affirmations disguised within the circumstances of my life. I would affirm this reality through my own obsessive behavior or actions. From the moment I would wake up to when I would fall asleep, I would lead a life of deception created by the constructs of my mind. Day after day I willingly surrendered to their rigid conditions, hoping that they would eventually leave me to live a life of anonymity.

Despite what I now know, I still catch myself reaffirming the absurdity of this reality. Therefore, I know how hard it will be for some of you to hear this Truth, much less accept the possibility that positive affirmations could change your life. The natural tendency will be to dismiss this practice entirely. However, in the new dream state, you will use your affirmations to remind you of your true identity, for the constructs of your mind will stop at nothing to convince you otherwise. Though you may experience frustration and fear, I assure you that as long as you remain steadfast with your affirmations, the walls between your inner and outer realities will crumble and the reign of the egoic mind will end.

I urge you to stay positive with your affirmations no matter how difficult it may be for you to do so. The world of duality will throw everything at you to test your resilience, not because of some evil illuminati who is planning your demise, but rather because of your obsession with believing one exists. Use the words "I Am" to affirm your Truth for its spiritual translation is that of God. Understand that your affirmations create a rhythmic energy so powerful that your reality can be overwritten – instantaneously! This is why mantras and chanting are so effective in manipulating energy to create a metaphysical response in your physical reality.

Even if you are not ready to accept the Truth behind your affirmations, recognize what is good in your life as often as you can. Be mindful of when and how you use the words I Am. For in the dream state it is far more likely that you will use I Am to affirm the negativity in your world. In doing so, you will unknowingly give credit to the darkness which will haunt you forever.

Focus & Determination

When Caleb came back into my life, there wasn't a week that went by where I wasn't absorbed in a Download or discussion that would last an hour or more. And yet, I didn't feel as though I was getting far enough with my desires for peace, love, happiness and spiritual freedom. There were no measurable outcomes to point to that would leave me feeling a strong sense of accomplishment. How was it possible that I could know so much, but yet see so little in return?

It wasn't until I was introduced to the Attributes that I began to realize that my entire life had been focused on things *out there*. That despite how determined I was to change my life, I was unwilling to focus that determination inward so that I could begin to address the fears that were preventing me from starting my inner quest. Looking back, it wasn't that I lacked the focus and determination to change my world, it was my obsession in wanting to direct those energies outward that prolonged my awakening and the desire for enlightenment.

In the old dream state, focus and determination are often used within the context of what we desire to achieve *out there*. Within the new dream state, we are asked to redirect these energies toward those things we want to achieve *in here* – that is to say, in our mind. In either case, humanity has often been accused of lacking these traits which has led to its perceived ineptitude. In fairness, the mind of the Left Brain Consciousness has performed brilliantly in its function to maximize our experience with duality. As I have stated before, the original dream state wasn't designed to offer us a road map to enlightenment.

In the new dream state, you will remember to block out all distractions of the mind and those of your five senses. You will remember that to be determined is to go beyond fear to a state of beingness where doubt no longer exists. You will remember how to use focus and determination in synchronicity for they are meant to complement each other. They are here to carve out a path by which you can experience your inner quest. Imagine them as your bodyguards determined to protect you from a world of distractions vying for your attention.

But make no mistake, their power is based upon where you stand relative to your faith and the source of your intentions. Therefore, use focus and determination to point you in the direction of that Truth. A direction that will lead you inward to the greatest quest you will ever experience in your life. Avoid the naysayers that will have you questioning the legitimacy of your conduct. Know that they have long since surrendered themselves to the endless maze of the original dream state.

"But that's insane," you will say. "I can't just walk away from my physical reality. I have much to lose if I focus everything inward." I assure you that you are already lost and that the only way back is to go inward. It will take a tremendous amount of focus and determination to stay the course, but in the end you will free yourself from the absurdity of this physical reality.

Intuition & Love

Despite my unwillingness to surrender to the Truth, there was always this sense of knowing that I could see beyond the perception of my physical reality. I could always rely on it to warn me if I was heading down a path I would inevitably regret. When I was a child I relied heavily on my inner Voice. I could feel its presence almost everywhere which provided me with a sense of security relative to the hauntings of my past. As I got older, however, this sixth sense or intuition would come to be used sparingly, if at all. It wasn't until my awakenings that I came to realize that my intuition was the physical manifestation of my higher Self. It was Caleb's way of staying in touch with me before I was ready to receive them into my life.

Therefore, never discard the importance of your intuition. Your intuition is your higher Self manifesting itself before you are willing or able to hear it as such. It is not petty nor is it negligible. For whoever tells you differently is doing so out of ignorance. Never doubt your intuition for it is here to serve as your compass, helping you to navigate through the unknown regions of your physical reality. It is a gift from you to you for the purpose of remembering you.

Your intuition allows you to tap into a state of beingness that transcends thought, knowledge or even wisdom. It is a direct communication of the God Consciousness and is often described as a "gut feeling" which should come as no surprise since the gut is also known as the "Second Brain." This explains why intuition was known to have inspired some of the greatest thinkers of our time. Many of whom have spoken publicly about its impact on both their physical and metaphysical realities.

Since your intuition is simply the manifestation of your inner Voice, it already knows what you desire. It will never lead you astray nor should you ever view it as an illusion of the mind such as the ego construct. It is there to inspire as much as it is to protect. In the new dream state, your intuition will become second nature to you. You will learn to trust it along with the other extra-sensory capabilities acquired through your heightened state of vibrational frequency.

In time, it will come to speak to you as Caleb does with me and the two will become inseparable. Like a genie in a bottle, it will be there whenever you call upon it. It will only be suppressed if you suppress it. Therefore, as your Attributes heighten, so will your willingness to listen to your intuition. Be cognizant of how you feel when your intuition is at play. Embrace it as your sixth sense and you will come to rely on it as much, if not more so, than your physical senses.

As for love, I leave the best for last for it represents all that we are and shall ever be. Love is substantially more than just a human emotion. It is the fabric by which we are woven into spiritual beingness. There is no energy more powerful than that which we know of as love. It is not limited or controlled by dimensionality nor is it restrained by the limitations of the dream state. It is nothing and yet everything to all and it exists unconditionally, now and forever.

Everything in our universe, be it seen or unseen, has some element of love in it. Therefore, to believe that you do not know love or have yet to experience it, is to recognize that you are asleep in the dream state. We have conditioned ourselves well to believe that love is a gift that only someone or something *out there* can give us. Sadly, we have wasted our lives searching for something *out there*, never realizing that it already defines who we are *in here.*

"How do you know this?" you will ask. "Your life hasn't been a bed a roses." I can't argue with that. I have spent a significant amount of time in search of love and will share that story in the next chapter. What I will tell you now is that I have been fortunate to experience a love like no other. And though I love my family and would give my life to protect them, the love I speak of is the one I felt in my near death experience. The vision I now recall as my Million Hugs. It is a love which penetrates every cell in the body, leaving you in a state of complete ecstasy. It is almost indescribable, yet that experience taught me that love makes up the core of who we are and that will never change.

In our physical world, love is the only energy that resonates from the heart to all of creation. Creation at any level, be it here or in any other dimension in or outside of this time-space reality, could not exist without love. Imagination could not exist without love. Its power to transcend reality is so deeply woven into our consciousness that in order to disguise love in the dream state, we created the illusion of an equally-powerful force in the form of fear. So good were we in losing ourselves in this illusion that fear has become the foundation of our human existence.

Nevertheless, in the dream state it is still possible to know yourself as love. To follow your heart rather than simply your mind when experiencing life. To recognize that it, along with your higher Voice, know you more than you know yourself. Remember that if the most beloved spiritual teachers of our time could achieve this insight, so can you! That is not to say that you will abandon your thoughts, but rather that you will allow them to be inspired by the energies of love. "But you are asking the impossible of me," you will say. "I have no idea what love is, much less how to use it to remember who I am." I know that for many this will be difficult to do, but I tell you that it does not have to be this way.

If you are here it is because you already know yourself to be more. You know that these words are resonating with the core of who you are and this core recognizes you as love. In time, you will approach your life from the stillness of that core. You will come to know love as the greatest state of beingness imaginable. Like intuition, you will come to trust it beyond your physical senses, knowing that love is in the vibrational signature of all energy.

When you are ready, you will come to use love as the greatest weapon among your Attributes. When situations arise you will ask confidently, "What would love do right now? How would it respond to the fears that reap havoc in my life?" Know that since you are love, you are simply asking your higher Self those questions. I assure you that if you start with the intention of love, your inner world will change dramatically. And since your outer world is a reflection of your inner reality, it too will come to reflect this Truth.

I cannot help but be reminded of *A Christmas Carol* where Scrooge, the main character in the story, finds his way back to the stillness of his inner world after realizing that love had not abandoned him. How he came to realize what was possible in his world once he could see himself from the perspective of love. From that day forward he was a new man and his life was reflected by the love he would share with a child named Tiny Tim. A love so great that it would change the course of their lives forever.

No other Attribute has changed my life more than love. It has given me purpose and a reference point by which to see my world. Along with all the other Attributes, I have been given everything needed to stay awake and ascend into a higher state of consciousness. All that remained was my willingness to "be still and know." To become that stillness of consciousness where I could exist as nothing and yet everything to all. To know that from that stillness I Am God and as such, everything is possible. A leap of faith greater than any other. A profound lesson that would have to be beaten into me time and time again before I would see the light and follow my Truth!

Chapter Six

Manifestation

A dear friend once told me that when it came to staying healthy, nutrition was 95 percent art and 5 percent science. I was shocked to hear that coming from a man who had devoted his life as a professor to the study of food science. Nonetheless, I never questioned his philosophy. As a result, my desire to create a nutrition company was born. Along with it, the creation of the most powerful superfood blends on the planet.

Manifestation is no different. I call it an art because it is. Notwithstanding, there is plenty of science behind it which I will leave for the next chapter. For now, know that to manifest is to immerse yourself in the art of emotion. Therefore, your role is to be the artist, leaving the science to the Universe. As the artist, you create through your desires, handing them off faithfully to the Universe to make them happen. But it is here where most of us get tripped up. Allow me to explain.

It seems like there's always something new coming out about manifestation relative to our desires for health, wealth and love. And though we came here to experience these things in our physical reality, the way in which we seem to be approaching the art of manifestation has left many frustrated with this endeavor. Intentional or not, those who are speaking to this issue are often directing our focus on the external results, rather than the internal process that is ultimately responsible for what we manifest.

Manifestation is no different than our desire for spiritual actualization. In other words, they both require us to direct our attention inward to a place few have dared to enter. It takes an enormous amount of discipline and practice to attain this inward focus, but I assure you the rewards are beyond anything you could achieve outwardly. Nevertheless, since we live in an action-oriented society, many will choose to follow the social construct, measuring their achievements by their ability to physically manipulate the world *out there*.

For years, I believed in the old adage that hard work was the way to personal success. I found it nearly impossible to think that techniques such as visualization or meditation could ever amount to much. They seemed so impractical in a world where every minute was a minute wasted if I wasn't working toward some measurable outcome *out there*. In my mind, there was no way I was going to achieve any level of success by sitting on some couch meditating or focusing on my inner world – or would I?

I will answer this question within the context of several Truths that have changed my entire view on manifestation. The first involves what I call the "Contract." The Contract is what we all agree to follow before coming into this physical reality. It sounds rather ominous but it really isn't. It is more of a lesson plan rather than any type of binding agreement. We use our Contract to list our expectations relative to the life we are about to live. In turn, the expectations provide our reasons for being here and the extent to which we care to be challenged in this lifetime.

It is important to know that you lay out these expectations. And that every expectation you have is simply to put into practice what you already know but have yet to experience, or have experienced but have yet to master in this physical reality. In general, we are all here to advance our spiritual beingness, but there are many who are now here for a greater purpose. A purpose I will discuss later in this book. Regardless of the reason, the more challenging you choose to make your life out to be, the more potential there is to manifest powerful desires.

In the original dream state, you came here to apply your lesson plan within the context of duality. The intent was to see how many ways you could experience yourself relative to your ability to achieve peace, love, happiness and spiritual freedom from within. In the new dream state, the intent is to experience yourself within the context of remembering. To remember "who" you are and "why" you chose to come at this time. To remember that your external world cannot change, nor does it necessarily have to, until you make the necessary changes from within.

"That seems like such a daunting task," you will say. "You must have the wrong person. I'm not capable of such feats." It wasn't that long ago that I felt the same way. I could barely manage to get out of bed, much less think that I could change my world by changing the inner me. I assure you that you are more than capable because in the world of consciousness, you are all masters of manifestation, you simply have forgotten. I have alluded to this before but I will briefly explain it again, for its importance to the manifestation process is immense.

In the original dream state, the Left Brain Consciousness serves as your gatekeeper. It is there to translate energy signals from your outside world that are transmitted to your physical senses. That translation creates thought which is then joined with some level of emotion to create a language based on feeling. A language which the Universe uses to create more of that reality. I need you to pause for a moment and re-read this paragraph as often as needed. For I am basically showing you the blueprint by which you, and only you, are creating this physical world you think is real. "You're crazy," you will say. Am I?

I challenge you to explore what your new sciences are discovering, not just with an open mind but with an open heart. To seek out the Truth in the teachings of the ancient traditions and in the original manuscripts of the greatest teachers and civilizations that have ever existed on our planet. It is there that you will find your Truth. That you are so much more than what you have been led to believe. That each and every moment that you exist, you are defying the laws of statistics by creating realities whose probabilities are almost immeasurable within the dream state.

> *"The probability is one," the Voice whispered as it greeted me the way it had many times before since my reunion with Caleb. It was becoming rather customary to hear Caleb's voice when waking up each day. I cannot tell you how much that meant to me. To know that I had that to look forward to each and every day made my life more bearable. For I was beginning to win my war with depression knowing that Caleb was by my side.*
>
> *"The probability is one," Caleb would keep repeating. "What are you talking about?" I would mumble under my breath as I tried to clear the cobwebs that had formed from the night before. Caleb avoided the*

question and just kept going with the morning mantra. You see this was Caleb's rather annoying way of making sure their point was being made and more importantly, understood.

"There are two ways to look at your reality," they proceeded. "You can look at reality from the perspective of the past to determine the probability of any future event occurring. Or, you can look at it from the possibility that each and every moment is independent of the last, and that you control the outcome of that moment. Therefore, the probability of any particular event occurring is one. One in one to be more exact."

As I sat there with my mouth open, I could feel the neurons in my brain rewiring themselves to align with this Truth. It was as if a bulldozer was clearing a path by which to understand this radical concept. I wish there was a better way to explain what I experienced at that moment, but it was as though all these symbols were being thrown at me to clear the way for a more enlightened consciousness to enter. Geometric symbols, patterns and mathematical equations were streaming everywhere, many of which I had never seen before. And just like that – it clicked!

That's not to say that my rational mind took this sitting down. "That's ridiculous," I could hear it screaming from somewhere deep in my head. "You don't believe this stuff, do you?" That was such a rhetorical question to ask. Of course I believed it, for one reason and one reason only — because it made sense! Not to my rational mind of course, but in my heart and in places deep within my soul it felt amazing. It was as though someone had just played the most beautiful melody I had ever heard. A sonata that left me in tears.

Caleb led me by the hand as if they had something more they wanted to share. In an instant, I found myself on a plane with Sharlene and the kids. We were preparing for liftoff when I heard the flight attendant say something in Spanish. Her voice shook me into the present moment as I found myself back in my body but unable to control it. I was merely an observer to an event that had already occurred in my life. Much like in a movie where the main character is thrown back into time to watch an incident unfold but is unable to do anything about it.

"Imagine everything that had to happen for this little baby, born in Colombia, to make his way to Minnesota," Sharlene would say as we both looked out the window as the plane took off. "Imagine all the people and all the events that had to occur for you to be here." I sat there for what seemed like an eternity contemplating what she had just said. I could feel the operating system in my mind as it searched for a convenient place to store this moment just in case I needed to reference it someday.

"The probability is one," Caleb would chime in as if to answer Sharlene's question for me. "How will you perceive your world? If you perceive your world to be contingent on the past, then you will always be a

> *prisoner of the dream state. If you choose, however, to see your world as a continuous stream of independent realities, then the probability of that child making it to Minnesota will always be one. The question then is not, 'Can an event occur?' But rather, 'Which event do you choose knowing what you know?'"*

Looking back, I remember feeling like a prize fighter who had just gone twelve, grueling rounds with an opponent who threw everything at me including the kitchen sink. I wasn't sure whether the temporary paralysis I was feeling was due to the astonishing information I had just received, or whether it was due to the fact that I actually understood it with tremendous clarity. Regardless, Caleb's point was extremely well taken and brilliantly placed within the context of duality. For Caleb was showing me two ways in which to see my world, not just in terms of probabilities, but also in how I viewed my relationship with duality. For the first time I could see how duality could play a role in reminding me of what I had forgotten, rather than simply being the demon I made it out to be.

Going forward, Caleb would introduce new concepts or new ways of thought that would challenge my view on life. It was as if a whole new world had opened up to me and I couldn't get enough. But despite all of the remembering, I still wasn't seeing the results in my physical reality. My world was still reflecting much of my past. I was trying so hard to embody what Caleb was saying only to have frustration meet me every step of the way. I began to question myself, wondering if I was making the same mistake again by listening to my inner Voice.

> *"Be still and know," Caleb's voice echoed as my mind drifted away from some obscure dream I was having. "What did you say?" I mumbled in my head. "Be still and know," Caleb responded. "Know what?" I*

asked, somewhat annoyed at Caleb for waking me up to yet another obscure mantra. A mantra they were determined to repeat for what seemed like an eternity.

"What is it that you want me to know?" I pleaded as my annoyance gave way to submission. Though somewhat befuddled by Caleb's behavior, I wasn't completely surprised. I had been despondent for days and though I was meditating quite frequently, I couldn't seem to quiet my mind long enough to communicate with Caleb. I was getting frustrated and disillusioned and I knew Caleb could sense that.

"You have passed the tipping point," Caleb would say in a rather nondescript manner. "What do you mean?" I asked, hoping to provoke some further explanation. "From this point forward, it will be easier for the Universe to manifest your desires. That is not to say that your desires will manifest instantaneously, but rather what you have wished for is now destined to become physical. You must learn, however, to 'be still and know.' To enjoy the unfolding of life before you."

Caleb's words left me speechless. All I could do was lay there quietly while they pontificated on what was to come and the choices I would have to make. "You are like a leaf floating down a stream whose destiny is clear now. There is no getting off this stream nor will you need to go against its current. You have done a fair amount of both in your life. But you have chosen to listen and in doing so, you have begun to look inward for the Truth."

"I don't know if I understand." I asked, as the initial shock began to wear off and I was beginning to feel both overwhelmed and overjoyed at the news. "What is it that I am supposed to do? And what did you mean by 'being still and know?'" I had just turned fifty-three and yet I felt like a little child who was taking his first steps. I wasn't sure how to embrace this new path. Was I ready to go on my own or did I need the familiar feeling of having someone's hand to hold on to?

"It is up to you as to how you want your path to unfold. How you want to reach your destination, for we assure you, you will reach it now. You may choose to make it more difficult, creating rapids and crashing into rocks along the way. Or, you may settle in and enjoy the serenity that comes along with surrendering to the steady flow all around you. It makes no difference to us nor will it to you. For in the end, you will reach your destination. In what manner and how quickly will be entirely up to you."

As if to overstate the point, Caleb started up again with the morning mantra. This time I wasn't bothered for I knew how important this message was relative to what laid ahead. I felt the words being etched in my brain as the heaviness in my heart disappeared. "Be still and know," I began repeating the words to myself. "Be still and know what?" I would ask myself in the months ahead. For now, however, my concerns were irrelevant as I knew Caleb had shared with me a Truth that was very sacred to my beingness and for that, I was eternally grateful. "Caleb, thank you so, so much. I will do my best to be still and know." And with that said, the transmission was done.

Little did I know that the inner quest I had been on for some time was about to take a much deeper turn in my life. A quest into the core of my beingness I knew I would eventually take. And though I was a bit scared at first, I found myself looking forward to more each and every day. As with most of my endeavors, I would choose to make my adventure down the river more difficult than it had to be. Rather than laying back and watching my life unfold as Caleb suggested, I would choose to make it treacherous by creating an abundance of stage four rapids along the way. Leaving me to hang on for dear life more often than not.

It would take the better part of a year before it would finally sink in as to the meaning of "be still and know." Ironically, the meaning was always there for me to see. It was simply a matter of understanding the messages that were hidden behind the very words that Caleb had used. To literally dissect each word, for they all contained clues that would help me from having to re-enter the chaotic world of the original dream state. I knew that if I were willing to live by those words, not just understand them, I would complete my transition into the new dream state of the Right Brain Consciousness. To do so, however, would require me to go deep within my faith to overhaul my entire belief system.

In the original dream state, I was introduced to faith as a means by which to develop a relationship with this being we call God. A relationship that would eventually determine the likelihood that this God would manifest my desires. In the new dream state, I started to see faith in a much different light. I began to see it as an expression of how I viewed myself. That is, the more I was willing to accept the possibility of a higher Self, the more I could feel my faith expanding into all areas of my beingness. It was there that I would learn to appreciate that faith was the glue by which the entire process of manifestation was held together. A lesson that would only become apparent to me when I allowed myself to "be still and know."

It was in my stillness that I began to see the obvious flaws within the way I approached the art of manifestation. I came to realize just how impatient and unwilling I was to appreciate the finer details that went into this process. That it was the art of getting there that would give me the most satisfaction in life. So great is this Truth that we have incorporated it into our current belief system of "no pain equals no gain." Yet, we have failed to apply this lesson to the most powerful and untapped resource we possess – our minds!

It was here that I came to understand that the rules were changing in this higher state of consciousness. That I was overlooking the fact that the new dream state operated very similar to my lucid dreams. That most of my frustration with deliberate manifestation had to do with the fact that I believed I was completely awake when in actuality, I was not. I was either just waking up or still asleep but thinking I was. Either way, to manifest within those two states of consciousness is nearly impossible unless I was willing to accompany it with extraordinary levels of physical action.

Remember that in the new dream state we are constantly drifting back and forth within various levels of the Right Brain Consciousness. That the more we are willing to remain within our stillness, void of any distraction, the longer we will remain awake. Then and only then can we create the momentum by which our true desires are manifested. Until then, we will continue to play this game of deception. Crying foul over the unjust rules of a world we created but have forgotten.

It is within that deception that many of you may have been told that to manifest your desires you need only to "ask," then "expect" and finally "receive." But if you listen closely enough, you will understand that there is more to this process that you already know but have forgotten. In fairness to those that are sharing their wisdom on manifestation, it is not that they are neglecting to speak to the entire process, but rather that we are unwilling or unable to hear the full message behind their teachings due to our perceived state of awakening. "So if what you say is true, how do I actually wake up?" you will ask.

The first thing you must do is accept that you have never left the silence. That the silence is who you are and that you are there right now. This is where your imagination comes into play. Even if the analytical mind refuses to believe such nonsense, use your experiential mind and allow your heart to take you home through your imagination. In doing so, you will bypass all the clutter and trappings of the ego construct to arrive safely in the one place where you are free to be your true Self. I cannot stress enough that this goes way beyond visualization, for what you are doing is accessing the inner world of your subconscious mind almost immediately. In other words, you are coming face-to-face with the authentic you who has been anxiously awaiting your return.

In the world of your imagination there are no limitations. You are not bound by any of the conditions you have placed upon yourself in the physical world. It is there where the canvass of your life is wiped entirely clean for you to express yourself in whatever way you desire. Therefore, to begin the manifestation process you must clear your mind so that you may focus your intention on being home again.

At first, you may find that you have brought back the heaviness of your external world. Know that in this place you call home, fear cannot exist for it vibrates at a much lower frequency. Use your imagination to shine your light on fear and watch how it dissolves into the loving energy it once was. In the metaphysical world of your inner consciousness, know that you are God and that all is possible when you hold your faith in the highest state of beingness.

It is in this stillness that you will ask for what is truly desired. For creation cannot be born anywhere else. It is here where you will summon the powers of your Attributes to give life to that which you will experience. Know that your desires will manifest themselves immediately in the metaphysical reality of your inner world. Have faith in knowing that this is your true reality and that what you see as your physical world is simply an illusion of your past. That in time, it too will reflect the Truth that you hold in your stillness. Know that the longer you hold that energy in your heart, the faster it will manifest in your outer world. Know this to be Truth and it will happen. Can you see now why your imagination is so critical to this process? Why it, along with all your other Attributes, were disparaged in the original dream state in order for you to experience duality?

Once you have immersed yourself in the metaphysical reality of what you desire, then and only then can you come from a place of pure expectation. You must learn to "feel" that desire in your imagination in order to set it free in your physical reality. Remember that this is your kingdom where you have full dominion of everything. Therefore, when asking you must come from a place of knowing where there is complete "understanding" of the beingness that is required. Can you see now how faith is woven into every element of your creation? That it cannot and never will be about thinking, wanting or hoping but rather knowing, understanding and becoming.

"Who cares if I can create a utopian world in my mind," you will argue. "What is that going to do for me out here? I'm dying out here and you are asking me to create fairytale worlds." I am telling you now that this is EXACTLY what you need to do. In the new dream state, you must use your imagination to be the bridge between the Left and Right Brain Consciousness. You must learn to first experience your desires from within before they can manifest themselves in your outer world. This is exactly why many of you are not living the life you desire. You are trying to do so by simply using the limited powers of your Left Brain Consciousness. In other words, you are trying to create from a place somewhere *out there* that simply does not exist.

This is the secret sauce that has been left out of many of your recipes. It is no wonder that you have labored so hard to see so little in return. I know I did, and that life almost killed me. Maybe not physically, but mentally and spiritually for sure. This is the Law of Resonance that I alluded to earlier. It is the Law that must come first before the Law of Attraction can be applied successfully. I know that it is mentioned in many of your teachings, but for reasons that should be obvious now, it too was shun from the original dream state.

"What are you implying?" you will ask. I'm not implying anything. Rather I am merely stating a fact. That in the original dream state we are conditioned to believe that no pain means no gain. And that by pain, it must involve some form of physical labor, and a lot of it. Therefore, by placing our attention somewhere *out there* we significantly diminish our ability to create a state of coherence between our inner and outer worlds. In doing so, we relegate our Universal Laws to the mundane task of repeating what we believe to be real through our physical senses.

In the new dream state, we will invite ourselves back to a place where synchronicities exist between both worlds. A place where the *outer* will finally reflect what is being experienced in the *inner,* rather than the *inner* reflecting the *outer* which is where most of you exist today. We will experience coincidences for what they truly mean. That is to say, the alignment of two things that match each other perfectly. How ironic is it that we have used the word "coincidence" to mean the exact opposite, when all along in its purest, mathematical sense it has always held a profound secret to our existence.

Know that the Law of Attraction has nothing to do with us creating our physical reality. But rather, it has everything to do with the alignment of two worlds whose beginning and end can only come from a place of resonance. Understand that in the metaphysical, everything is limitless. Therefore, everything that has ever been thought of already exists in some aspect of dimensionality. And, what does not yet exist is being born through our desires. That this was the sole purpose for experiencing duality. For we are not here to simply enjoy the experience of physicality, but also to revel in the further expansion of our inner consciousness.

At this point, I am compelled to sum up, for these points are too significant to overlook. To begin with, to "deliberately" manifest you must do so from a place of stillness. A place you have never left and one where you and only you have access to. It is a place where fear cannot exist. And it can only be accessed through your imagination which enables you to bypass the pitfalls of your egoic mind. It is there where your imagination will run freely to create whatever brings you peace, love, happiness and spiritual freedom, for those are the purest intentions we have as spiritual beings.

You will summon your Attributes to assist you as you surrender to the beingness of that experience. To feel with all your heart and soul the love and creation of your imagination. In doing so, you will allow yourself to hold that energy long enough for the Universe to bring you its physical equivalent. Then and only then will the Law of Attraction work for you in the manner you have always desired. Then and only then will your two worlds become Oneness.

Understand that all of this requires the highest level of faith in yourself. That you can, if only for the purpose of imagining, know yourself as that which you are and will always be. That you possess not only the secret by which to achieve your awakening, but also the physical manifestation of your true desires. That one must follow the other if you are going to use the Laws of the Universe correctly. Know that you have never been alone in this endeavor and that the voice you are listening to, as you read this book, is your Voice which is calling you to greatness. It has been preparing you for this day and has gifted you with the Attributes to do so in whatever manner you desire to start your quest.

Know that you do not have to be fully engaged in the practice of manifestation in order to alter your physical reality. You are doing so every day without even knowing it. Albeit, through the limited capacity of the Left Brain Consciousness. Nevertheless, your Attributes are always there to help you access the more awakened state of the Right Brain Consciousness. At times, their presence is so subtle that it will appear as though they are nonexistent in your life. However, if you look carefully you will see how they have woven themselves so brilliantly into some of the most defining moments of your life.

> *At twenty-six, I was trying to live a rather unassuming life relative to my spiritual pursuits. That's not to say that I wasn't cognizant of my inner Voice. There wasn't a week that went by where I wasn't reminded of some deeper purpose I was here to fulfill. Nevertheless, I had made a choice a few years earlier to channel that energy into other endeavors. I had recently moved to Minnesota and had begun to see a future there. As such, I decided to redirect my focus toward laying down some roots in the hope of finding answers somewhere "out there."*

Upon arriving, I found a new passion in my life which was to be a full-time student in college. A somewhat humorous twist in my life since I wasn't much of an exemplary student growing up. In fact, I once held the dubious honor of earning a grade so low that it didn't even exist in the school's grading system. Yet, here I was years later enjoying the life of a graduate student and loving every minute of it.

Within a few years, I had a growing circle of friends but no real love interest that I could see "long term" in my life. This was rather disconcerting since love had always been a central theme in my upbringing. Growing up, I could always rely on my mother's unwavering love no matter the circumstances. My father would try as well, but doing so came harder for him since love wasn't always reciprocated by his father; especially as they both got older.

I also knew that love was key to what was happening in my inner world. But since I wasn't ready to explore its inward meaning, I chose the path of least resistance by searching for love in all the wrong places. Not surprisingly, throughout my late teens and into my twenties, I struggled mightily with relationships. Often times, coming face-to-face with insecurities I had never personally experienced as a child. Feelings that I acquired along the way from empathic abilities that were still foreign to me at the time.

As if that weren't enough, I couldn't find a sympathetic ear to save my life. Everywhere I turned, it was always the same advice, "Don't worry, you'll figure it out."

Or my favorite, "It's all a part of growing up," as if this were some rite of passage into adulthood that everyone was required to go through. Looking back, I should have realized that those who were giving me advice were as clueless as I was since we were all still asleep in the dream state.

By the time I started graduate school, I couldn't care less what reality I was living in. I couldn't find love if it were standing right in front of me. Yet, another twisted irony I would come to appreciate later in life when I discovered that everything in my world had elements of love in it. Therefore, in actuality love had been standing there all along, I was just too blind to see it.

Nevertheless, I was determined to give it my all. I looked everywhere for love, coming close in some instances, but missing the mark with most. There wasn't a stone I hadn't turned over. In my frustration, I began placing similar expectations on my friendships. I was feeling defeated and just wanted to feel worthy of someone's attention. In all cases, my intentions were all wrong. As a result, I began to suffer from it both mentally and spiritually.

"What the hell am I doing?" I would ask repeatedly, as I laid in bed for hours before falling asleep. "Why am I so obsessed in finding love? I just want to stop feeling this way." Since I had shut myself off to my inner world, I had no choice but to deal with this on my own. Thank goodness Caleb wasn't in agreement. Though it would take some doing, Caleb was always

there for me. Always finding a way to settle things down long enough to show me the way.

I knew that the drama of my outer world was a symptom of a greater problem lurking in the shadows of my inner beingness, waiting for the right moment to strike. That my world was simply mirroring the inner chaos of a life that had seen too much pain along the way. I knew that both worlds were on a collision course and that it was up to me to stop that from happening, if only for a while. As such, I reluctantly raised the white flag and began an open line of communication with my inner Voice.

One day, something rather unexpected happened. I remember waking up to one of my favorite songs being played on the radio. I recall thinking how unusual it was that it was being played since it didn't quite fit the format of that station. Since my mind was rather clear, I allowed the lyrics to run freely in my head. Within a few seconds, it occurred to me that a specific message was being formed from somewhere deep within.

The message came in crystal clear as the lyrics hit me right between the eyes. It was about the freedom of self-expression and our desire to live life without limitations. I laid there soaking it all in. Watching as these lyrics went to work reconnecting areas of my mind that had laid dormant for years. I knew, right then and there, that I had to make my inner world work if I was going to find peace, love, happiness and spiritual freedom in my life. Without giving it much thought, I set sail that morning into the outer regions of my inner world. Little did I know that it would be another twenty-five years before I would be ready to navigate my way back into its inner core of silence.

The holidays were fast approaching and I was really looking forward to going home and seeing family. School was going well and in keeping with my new resolution, I had just ended a relationship with a wonderful young woman who couldn't have been more supportive of my desire to sort things out in my life. A life she knew she wouldn't be a part of. It was the first time in years that I was truly happy and eager to see what life had in store for the three of us – that is, me, myself and I. Just as I was beginning to appreciate this new found friendship with my inner world, the unexpected came to visit me yet again.

A few days before I had planned on leaving for Chicago, I got a call from two of my dearest friends who couldn't wait to tell me that their holiday party was back on again. A party that had become somewhat legendary among those who knew it well, but whose certainty that year was questionable due to so many conflicting schedules.

Though they knew of my plans to go home early for the holidays, they were both relentless in their determination to have me there. They had perfectly orchestrated this conversation knowing that I would be no match for their witty banter. And so, after about thirty minutes or so I threw in the towel and decided to stay. A decision that would change my life forever.

Going into that party, I had no expectations other than to enjoy a spectacular night with some great friends. I arrived early which was unprecedented for me, to say the least. I wasn't planning on staying late because I still had some packing to do since I was leaving the next morning to go home. Little did I know that I was just minutes away from one of the most defining moments of my life.

"Look up dummy, there she is!" the Voice would shout out somewhat hysterically in my ear. I was completely taken back by the Voice who appeared to have come out of nowhere. You see, I had been standing by myself near the pool table for quite some time, watching intently as the festivities unfolded. Not recognizing the Voice, I immediately turned to see who was standing next to me only to find there was no one there. Seemingly perplexed, I paused for a moment but was soon distracted by the young ladies who were making their way in from the outside.

I knew immediately who this Voice wanted me to see. For right before me stood this vision of beauty I had never witnessed before. As if I were being prodded to do the unthinkable, I immediately walked over to greet our new guests. "Welcome to my party," I said, as I couldn't take my eyes off of this woman who had me before she could even say "hello."

"My name is Franco and I'm one of the hosts. If you need anything just let me know." Of course it was a bold face lie since I wasn't one of the hosts. But honestly, I didn't care because I knew it was love at

> *first sight. The fairytale that I had always wanted from years of listening to my mother talk about her Prince Charming. The one she let get away years before meeting my father. The "happy ever after" I was told didn't exist in this world but was now standing right in front of me.*
>
> *As fate would have it, Sharlene would feel the same way. Before the night was over, she would give me a list of telephone numbers I could reach her at. Everything from her work, to her parents, to where she was living at with her two roommates, were fair game. Suffice it to say, it didn't take long for me to call her after the party.*
>
> *I came back to Minneapolis right after Christmas, and as the clock struck midnight on New Year's Eve, we had our first kiss. A few years later, I would get on one knee and on that very spot where we met, I would ask this angel to marry me. I thank God, for on that day she said yes. And unbeknownst to me, she freed me to a love that would flow abundantly in my life, forever!*

Looking back, I sit here in awe at the role my Attributes played in making love a reality in my life. The crazy thing is, I didn't even know it at the time. The years I spent imagining my soulmate and the feelings I would have when meeting her would all come to pass. Caleb's determination to speak to me through a song weeks before the party would turn out to be instrumental in my realization that I had to go inward to find true love. I think back to the excitement and awareness I felt as my intentions shifted from fear to love. I can still feel the eagerness I had to begin my first expedition into an inner world I knew nothing of.

I remember being so focused and determined not to let anyone or anything get in my way. I was grateful and appreciative of the life I had and began to see my world with compassion rather than disdain. I was so confident that I would find love within that this feeling of anticipation began to overtake every cell in my body. I was happy and I wasn't afraid to express my emotions to anyone. Most of all, I was willing to put my ego aside and allow this Voice to guide me to wherever I needed to go. In return, the Universe was able to give me everything I had ever wanted and more when it came to this state of beingness called love.

I want you to know that it doesn't have to take years for something to manifest in your life. In my case, it took that long only because I refused to use my Attributes to create anything other than the prison walls of my mind. I wasn't willing or able to use my imagination to bypass the infested waters of my world in order to seek refuge in the serenity of my silence. But when I finally did, the Universe was free to begin its work in mirroring my outer world with who I really was inside.

I know there are some of you that are looking for a miracle right now. Know that miracles are simply our "intense" willingness to focus every ounce of every Attribute on our desires from a place of silence. A place so impenetrable that doubt would never dare show its face. Since most of us are unwilling or unable to enter such silence on our own accord, the opportunity to manifest a miracle often presents itself when we are dealt with a calamity. We have all heard of such miracles, from the mother who defied all reason and science to lift up a car to save her child, to the miraculous recovery of those dealing with life threatening conditions or illnesses.

I assure you that in each instance, the power of our Attributes came into play. That people, no different than you and me, used that power to transport themselves to a place where the unthinkable could come true, if only for a few precious moments. The same precious moments my mother used to call upon her Attributes to save my life when I was an infant dying of pneumonia. The same precious moments that saved my son's life when he ran into the oncoming traffic to hug me at the airport. And the same precious moments that gave Sharlene's father another chance at life when she prayed for his recovery from cancer from a place of silence she knew nothing of but somehow managed to summon.

Know that you are more than capable of performing such miracles. In fact, you are all capable of so much more! It is time now for you to listen to that inner Voice which has been calling you to greatness. Imagine what lies ahead when you are finally ready to start your quest into the inner world of you. That moment when you are ready to say, "No!" to all the distractions of your outer reality. To say, "It's time to be the authentic me I came here to be!" Imagine what you will accomplish when you are finally ready to see the artist that you truly are.

Though I said your role is that of an artist, there is one more thing you need to know. That is, you need to know the Truth as it relates to the 5 percent of science I referred to early on. The portion of manifestation I call the "Game." For it represents the virtual reality within which all of what we know as our universe exists.

Some of you may not be ready to hear what I am about to tell you. You will do everything to downplay its significance, while others will simply walk away. But I assure you, it is absolutely critical that you understand its importance relative to the dream state. For if you are to find your way out of this maze you call "life," you must come to know the Game you have been playing since the day you were born!

Chapter Seven

The Game

There has been much for you to absorb in this book. To know yourself as God can be a very daunting proposition. Nevertheless, I am here to tell you that the days of carrying your cross are over. That it is time to let go and surrender to the Truth that you came here to free yourself from a game you have been playing for far too long. That you came, not just to remember, but to share what you know so that others might do so as well.

I have shared what is required of you to break this cycle. Now it is time for you to know the Truth regarding the only world you have known since birth. A world created entirely out of your imagination to serve as a place of learning. Not just learning for the sake of learning, but rather learning for the sake of remembering. A school equipped with spiritual teachers to guide you along the way. But not just any school, a performing arts school where you are given the opportunity to experience the plan you created before coming here in physicality.

I want you to imagine that this school contains within it an even smaller environment. An environment known as the Game, for it is meant to be exactly that. It is the most sophisticated, virtual reality game imaginable. A holographic universe built by you, for you, so that you could come to experience yourself as God in every imaginable way possible. I know it will be easy to imagine such a world, but accepting it as your reality may be another matter altogether.

I am going to ask you to suspend your beliefs as I share what will be the most inconceivable Truths so far. Truths that will require you to surrender to your imagination. To let go of what your rational mind will tell you so that you can be free to follow the impulses of your heart. That being said, your analytical mind is free to wonder as well. I encourage you to allow it to explore the complexities of the Game for they are nothing less than extraordinary.

If you are not technically inclined, know that it is not necessary for you to understand the intricacies of the Game. Approach the Game like you would your car, phone or television. None of which you know relative to their complexities and yet, you use them every day with precision, grace, and in many cases – mastery. What is more important is that you have a general understanding of how the Game works, since I assure you it will help in taking back the controls of your world. As you come to master the Game, it will reveal more of its secrets so that you may come to know and appreciate its ability to help expedite your ascension into the higher dimensions of consciousness.

As we venture together into this sacred space, I ask that you keep an open mind and heart to the possibility that the Game may contain the answers you have been seeking. For once the seed of knowledge is planted, the flower will grow. To that end, I will share some fascinating insights that are meant to give you a brief but remarkable tour of the Game. I will also share what has been shown to me relative to our schooling here on earth. I will do so within the context of its role in our spiritual awakening which is now underway.

Know that I do not have the answers to all of its intricacies. Not in this present form nor in the present frequency within which I reside. That will come to all of us in time. For now, understand that we are being shown what we need to know to navigate our way through the Game and out of the dream state. As such, the intent is to have you approach the Game with as much clarity as possible. To help you avoid its pitfalls, which you have seen from my experiences, can be rather unpleasant.

To begin with, you must understand that you have reached a point in your spiritual evolution where it is time for you to wake up. A Truth that wants nothing more than to be revealed no matter how inconvenient it may be for you to accept. One that is prepared to push you to the brink of insanity for the sake of freeing you from yourself. In this vein, you must understand that the rules of the Game are also evolving to insure that this secret is exposed. No longer are you here to experience duality for the sake of contrast, but rather for the sake of remembering.

Know that the Game is here to help you view duality as your companion rather than your most hated nemesis. In doing so, you will come to see the riddles and clues that have been hidden all along behind so many of its messages. Avoid the temptation of discarding them for they are messages from your higher Self determined to communicate with you at all cost. You will see these messages everywhere but none more so than in the Voice you will hear in your mind, heart and soul. A Voice you know affectionately as your intuition.

Know that you too are experiencing an upgrade of the mind to prepare you for the Truths that lie ahead. Though it may not feel this way at first, I assure you that you will be more equipped to handle these Truths than you will be to avoid them. Hence, why many of you are now finding it difficult to run from their calling. For you have always been wired to understand these Truths but have simply forgotten. To be fair, it is not that you have forgotten, but rather that you have not had the necessary Downloads by which to awaken areas of the mind that have been kept dormant. In the months and years ahead, you will. That is of course if it hasn't already happened. Which for many reading this book – it already has!

It is also imperative that you understand that the mind is not some abstract place or function housed somewhere in the brain. In fact, it is not a creation of the brain at all, but rather just the opposite. That is to say, the brain is but one manifestation of the mind. Albeit, a significant one for it, along with both the Right and Left Brain Consciousness, resides in the same region of the body. Notwithstanding, the mind is located in and around your "entire" body. Concentrating its energies in other equally important regions you know as the gut and heart. In fact, in the world of metaphysics, the mind and consciousness are one, and therefore the mind is everywhere.

As I have already stated, though I will cover certain technical elements of the Game, I urge you to approach this discussion primarily from the experiential mind rather than its analytical counterpart. For in its purest sense, Consciousness does not operate in linear terms. I understand that this too runs contrary to what we have been taught to perceive. But I assure you that the only aspect of "mind" that functions this way is your Left Brain Consciousness. A consciousness that has struggled at times to rationalize, in linear terms, the pathological and often moronic behavior of both the ego and social construct.

I am asking more specifically that you suspend your belief that everything you see, hear, taste, smell or touch is real, for it is not. I understand that I have made this point many times before, but I feel that we are now at its apex. As such, I will attempt to explain this Truth within the context of the Game. Let me begin by stating that the world you see only appears to be real given your ability to use your physical senses to translate energy into matter. Therefore, what lies before and after the Now exists only as an illusion of the mind.

"Wait a minute," you will say. "Are you telling me that everything in my world, other than what I am experiencing right now, is not real? That's insane." That is exactly what I am saying. In fact, I will go one step further in stating that what you are experiencing in the present moment of the Now is simply a holographic creation of the mind. Therefore, everything – past, present and future – is an illusion. The Truth is that what you know of as matter is in actuality, energy in motion. Therefore, energy has and always will precede matter. In fact, whether you see it or not, everything in the universe is an expression of energy.

This gets back to one of my original premises that energy has no beginning nor does it have an end. It is here, there and everywhere. As such, every facet of who you believe to be is simply energy in motion. It is only in the present moment of the Now that energy comes to know itself as matter. The Now is the manifested stillness of time where the metaphysical and physical meet. It is directly correlated to the stillness of your mind. As such, it serves as a powerful portal connecting your two worlds. Only through stillness can energy go in and out of either reality.

In the physical world, for energy to transform itself into matter, it must begin by moving in a clockwise direction. As its speed increases, it will rise, creating a vortex whose spin gets tighter and tighter as it reaches the stillness of the Now. At which point the energy implodes and begins to slow down in an ascending, counterclockwise manner. Eventually it slows to the point where it becomes matter. But if the story were to end there, the holographic picture would be incomplete. For there are at least three critical pieces that have yet to be shared with most of humanity.

The first is simply a further refinement of my previous point. I have shown that matter is simply energy in motion but have yet to discuss the space within which it resides. It is widely known, at least within science, that 99.9999 percent of an atom is made up of empty space. What is less known and therefore highly debated, is whether or not anything exists in that space. A similar debate existed, until very recently, regarding the "blackness" of space which consists of 68 percent dark energy and 27 percent dark matter. The remaining 5 percent being matter as we have come to know it.

Through advancements in science, we are now able to detect a highly-sophisticated network of energy crossing throughout the universe in what was once thought to be empty space. Even more fascinating is the remarkable resemblance between this network and the neural network of our own bodies. Since matter is primarily empty space, isn't it possible that at the subatomic level such a network might also exist? The answer is most definitely yes! Therefore, it stands to reason that these networks are all somehow connected to one another. And if so, they must all behave similarly to our own network which serves as a pathway by which to manipulate energy into matter based on some form of stimulus. But what form would that be?

This gets to the second piece that was left out of the holographic picture. That is how, or better yet, who is manipulating this energy? On the surface, this would appear to be a no-brainer since we have been taught from birth to believe that this being, known as God, is the sole creator of our universe. But if that is true, wouldn't energy in its purest form be subjugated to God and only God's will when manifesting itself into matter?

The answer is "yes" it should, but the reality is "no" it does not since matter at the subatomic level appears to behave differently when being observed. In other words, when matter is being observed it behaves in a manner consistent with what the observer expected to see. But when it is not being observed, it behaves more like a frequency of energy. Therefore, at the subatomic level, which is where all physical creation begins in the stillness of the Now, energy is manipulated by the observer. And since you are the observer, it goes without saying that you are God!

It was a beautiful, summer day as I sat looking out at the trees in my backyard. I was in the midst of a significant Download and wanted to take full advantage of this open portal to get closure on questions that had haunted me for years. "Caleb, what happened that day at the airport?" I asked, still puzzled by an event that had happened years before.

"Did I actually see what I saw?" I wondered as if maybe it had all been a dream that had washed itself onto the shores of my lucid mind. "What happened that day when Logan almost died? Did everything actually stop or did I just imagine it? And if it did stop, what did it all mean?"

"Close your eyes," the Voice whispered as it began its transmission once more. I did as I was told and for a moment there was nothing but darkness. Just then, however, I could see in the distance what appeared to be a small, shining object materializing out of thin air; spinning in a somewhat unorthodox manner as if it were free to roam in whatever direction it pleased.

The object came closer and to my surprise it was a three-sided pyramid. "This is what keeps your world together," Caleb continued. "It acts as a force field capturing the energy signatures that are consistent with all of your feelings and desires. Everything that is physical exists within this force field. It is tuned to your consciousness and responds only to its language. A language that resonates from the heart. Therefore, when you draw your energy inward it does the same. When you express that energy outward, it reflects that expression in physicality.

"From where you stand, this symbol creates the holographic image you know as your universe. It is no different than the pixels you see on your television screen. Know that everything has its own pixel. Therefore, you as energy are a pixilation of the world around you. Just as your cells are a pixilation of you. Or, how an atom is a pixilation of each cell. This process is limitless and exists within the inner and outer realities of your world. Therefore, what happens to one, happens to all."

To say that I was floored by this Truth would have been an understatement. In a matter of seconds, Caleb had just explained humanity's relationship to itself and everything else in the universe. In simple terms, the universe was simply a holographic game expressing the desires of consciousness at every imaginable level.

But I could feel that there was something more Caleb wanted me to see. As I stood there contemplating the implications of what I had just heard, I began to sense the presence of something even greater. A level of frequency or beingness I hadn't felt before – not even in my dreams.

"Did you feel that?" Caleb would ask, knowing full well that I had. "That is your God Consciousness that experiences all perspectives, not as an 'either-or' dilemma, but rather as one 'concurrent' reality. It senses the Truth within every dimension that is spoken. It can do this because you are the sum of everything that is divinity. That is, you as Consciousness know yourself to be the 'Me, My-Self and I' which is always expressed as the One.

"The 'Me' being that which you have always known yourself to be as the limited body, mind and soul. The 'My-Self' being that which you know yourself to be as Spirit or the higher Self. And the 'I' being that which you are now remembering yourself to be as the I Am. Each one representing a corner of the pyramid. Therefore, what you desire from within will always be expressed through the physical manifestation held within this symbol. For it holds the codes within which all of creation is held together based on your desires. Change your expression and you change the codes. Change the codes and you change your world. This is the Universal Law of the 'Divine DNA.'" (see Figs. 7.1 through 7.3).

The Divine DNA

The Building Block of All Physical Reality

Figure 7.1

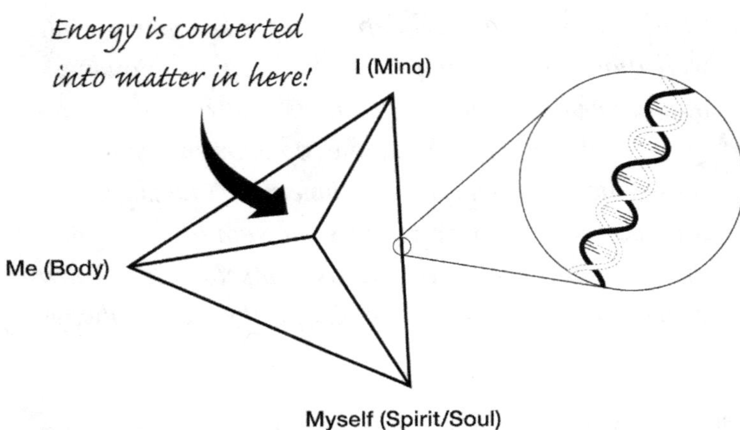

Digital Creation in the 3rd Dimension

In the Game, the holographic universe contains an extensive network that is identical to our biological neural network. These networks are all interconnected and send energy signals to their respective DNA structures which are then translated to create your physical reality. These signals are formed as a response to the electromagnetic field generated by the heart chakra (see, Chapter Four). In the original dream state, we operate under a limited state of consciousness known as the egoic mind. Therefore, when recognizing ourselves as the Me, Myself, and I, the mind is limited to the narrow perspective of the body, mind and soul. The energy signatures (i.e., codes) generated by the egoic mind are designed to reinforce the physical reality of the 3rd dimension. As such, abstract concepts such as the mind and soul are often discarded as inconsequential to the creation of physicality. (Note: The double helix structure of the pyramid (i.e., tetrahedron) which is identical to the double helix of our cellular DNA.)

The Divine DNA

The Building Block of All Physical Reality

Figure 7.2

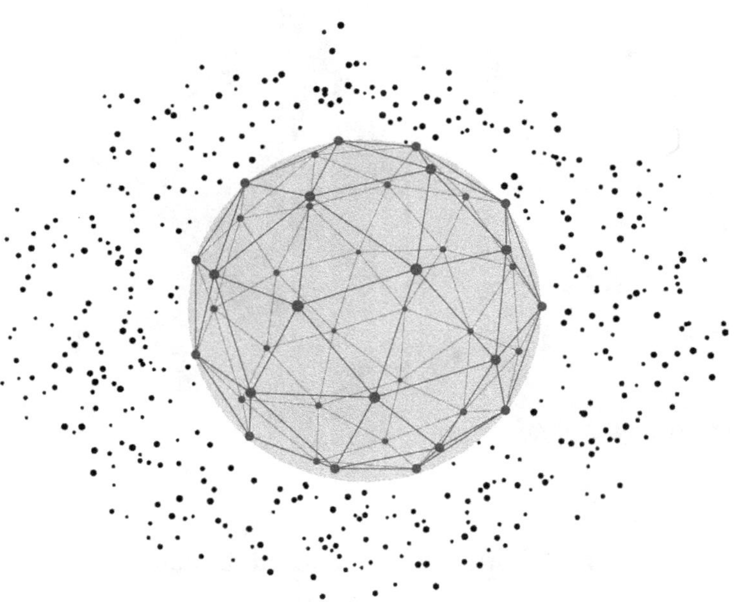

Digital Creation in the 3rd Dimension

The universe is an amalgamation of tetrahedrons that are created by our energetic expressions. It, along with the metaphysical world, are constantly expanding as we create new feelings and desires that are unique to each one of us. The exterior dots represent the continued expansion of our physical universe as metaphysical energy transforms itself into 3rd dimensional energy and matter.

The Divine DNA

The Building Block of All Physical Reality

Figure 7.3

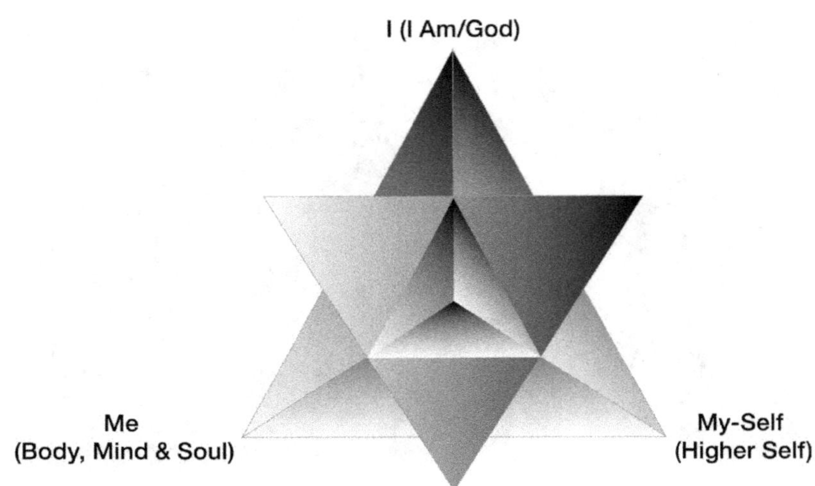

Digital Creation in the 4th & 5th Dimensions

In the new dream state (i.e., 4th dimension), you as Consciousness awaken to the realization of the higher Self known as the "My-Self" which creates a blended state of feelings and desires. In the awakened state of God Consciousness (i.e., 5th dimension), you begin to know yourself as nothing and everything to all. Otherwise, known as the "I Am" or God. These higher frequencies of consciousness change the genetic expression of what is released by the heart chakra. Consequently, these expressions change the genetic coding (i.e., sequencing) of the Divine DNA. Change the expression and you change the codes. Change the codes and you change your world. (Note: In certain instances, the tetrahedron evolves into a Merkaba, which when activated, creates a powerful spinning vortex and/or portal that enables one to connect to Source as Origin and the multidimensional frequencies of the multiverse. This symbol has been found in ancient manuscripts and monolithic structures all over the world, almost as if they had been left behind as a clue for us to uncover.)

I was completely lost in the moment and honestly, didn't know what to say. On the one hand, I was stunned that I knew exactly what Caleb was saying relative to the Divine DNA, but on the other, I had no idea what this had to do with what happened at the airport. I could feel my analytical mind taking copious notes as if to correlate what Caleb had just described with the events of that day.

"The moment you saw your child in danger, you summoned us – your higher Self," Caleb finally continued. "Sensing your urgency, we drew every bit of energy inward as your emotions came bursting out in the only manner available to you. In that instant, you changed the expression of your beingness with such conviction that everything in your time-space reality came to a halt. You yelled 'No!' and the universe knew to stop, which is exactly what happened!

"Nothing could withstand the emotional discharge of that moment. Time and space became irrelevant. You did not ask nor did you plea for the Universe to intervene, for deep down inside you knew what needed to happen. You did not want your child to die and to do that you had to suspend time and space. Every element at your disposal was focused on that child, and in that precise moment you changed the expression of your beingness, which in turn, changed the coding all around you.

"Remember, every expression has its own frequency. A frequency that can only originate from the heart. It is a harmonic frequency that contains a binary

coding system full of zeros and ones that pulsate in the same rhythmic manner as your heart. It is the same rhythmic pattern that is found deep within the core of your planet. In fact, it is found everywhere in nature and throughout the universe.

"This is the language of the Universe. It is not a language of words, but rather sounds that have a harmonic pulse to them. They emanate through energy, but if you were to hear them they would create an endless stream of tones. This language contains a science within it that has yet to be discovered in your world. It is based solely on the 'Science of Consciousness' and whose written language is just now being introduced into your world.

"What you saw that day all of you have seen before. It is part of your schooling but you do not remember. For you saw your physical reality as it truly is rather than what you perceive it to be. You saw it as a two dimensional screen or veil that appeared to have no beginning and no end. A pixelated screen based on what you perceived to be real as consciousness. One that would become three dimensional when interacting with the physical senses. Alter your senses and you change your expression. Change your expression and the screen will do whatever you desire. Which is exactly what happened to you that day."

Caleb wasn't always this detailed when responding to my questions. Even when they were, it was often explained in more spiritual terms. I knew I had hit on something that Caleb had been wanting me to ask. When I finally mustered up the courage to do so, they were ready to download everything I wanted to know and then some. It would take many more conversations with Caleb to fully appreciate and understand what was shown to me that day, but in time I began to unravel the mystery behind the Game.

Caleb opened my eyes to a Universe whose possibilities were truly endless. A Universe that was there to serve me if I could only get out of my own way. They had given me more than just a glimpse of the Game, but it was still up to me to do something with it. Ironically, I'm not much for puzzles but piecing together this Truth has been one of the most exhilarating experiences of my life. For each piece provided me with yet another clue as to the purpose of my existence; an enticement which kept me coming back for more. As if uncovering the Divine DNA wasn't enough, I knew I was on the brink of yet another major breakthrough that would turn every paradigm in my world right-side-up again.

Despite the many Downloads, there was still something missing but I couldn't put my finger on it. Caleb had shown me the secret behind the sequencing of the Divine DNA. I was also shown the neurological network of the universe that fed directly off of the electrical impulses of my emotions. I knew that those impulses created a harmonic language used by us as Consciousness to communicate with the Universe. That this language of sound represented some form of advanced mathematics, and although foreign to me, was now being discovered in patterns or sequences throughout nature and in many of the monolithic structures of our ancient civilizations.

It was here that I stumbled upon the third piece that had been left out of the holographic picture. You see throughout my many discussions with Caleb, I began to pick up a familiar theme in many of their messages. There were actually two themes but one was more blatant than the other. The most obvious theme had to do with energy frequencies and portals, the latter being a function of the former.

As for the less obvious theme, let's just say that it was a gut feeling that led me to ask the million dollar question which opened my world to a plethora of new information. An astounding assortment of data that would lead me to the Truth regarding the multi-dimensional world of the Game and the breakthrough I had been looking for.

> *"Caleb, can you tell me how the Game is played?" I asked, wondering if they would even know what game I was referring to. I had to ask since it was a question that had been on my mind for some time. I wasn't sure why, or for that matter, if it meant anything relative to my quest. I closed my eyes to see if Caleb would reply. Instead, my mind drifted back to the library where the Akashic Records were held and where my first awakening began.*
>
> *Without having to be told, I grabbed my book and headed straight to the reading room where I was greeted by two angelic figures standing near the doorway. The room was filled with others who were completely oblivious to my presence, sitting in what seemed to be a comatose state of mind. Heads fully immersed in the glow radiating from each book.*
>
> *I sat down and immediately joined them as a stream of white light penetrated my consciousness, making its way through every crevice of my beingness. In seconds, a sequence of glowing symbols, numbers and other geometric patterns began streaming across my mind like a parade of Christmas ornaments on a tree. There was one, however, that caught my attention*

immediately. It was a three dimensional expression of numbers one would see on a graph when two lines intersect to form four even quadrants. Given what was flashing all around, I was rather surprised that this simple graph would have captured my fascination.

"This is the 'Game' you call your life," Caleb whispered. "But all I see are two lines drawn on some sort of 3-D image that looks like graph paper," I replied, somewhat cynically. "Look closer and you will see more," Caleb was quick to respond. As the image drew closer I could no longer see its vertical line. In fact, it came in so quickly that I could feel myself being drawn into its imagery. I looked down and could now see that the horizontal line was streaming beneath me like a runway would to an airplane, as if it were trying to guide me in for a landing.

I braced myself for the impact but instead, everything came to a screeching halt some thirty feet or so above it. I looked down again only to realize that the line had turned into a strip of film that stretched as far as the eye could see. But it wasn't just any film, it was a film that contained my life – its past, present and future. "Understand that your life is the Game. It is not meant to be taken as a metaphor. You have been led to believe that this game unfolds in a linear manner but it does not," Caleb explained as their voice echoed from somewhere high above. "Even here it appears that way but look closely and we will show you, it does not.

"Imagine you are a conductor on a train and the film you see below is now its tracks. You are riding along letting it take you wherever it may go. Your life appearing to be a series of both random and seemingly structured events. On the surface it would seem to be a very linear path. But the Game is not that simple nor would you want it to be. For there exists an endless stream of paths continuously veering off from the original track. Some veering to the left while others to the right. Every thought and emotion you have dictating whether or not you stay on course. The change may be subtle, yet every variation could have tremendous implications on your life going forward.

"It gets even more interesting because the Game is designed to take you in any direction at any time. Therefore, these tracks can veer off into multiple plains of reality, for they can shoot out in any direction. They can go up, down and all around. And though you may not be able to go backwards given the frequency of your physical reality, you can and often do so in your metaphysical world. Causing you to live the present as if you were still in the past. The worse, however, is when you pull from the past to shape your future all while still in the present. Forcing you to draw from two energies that don't even exist in your physical reality. Leaving you to wonder why things never change in your life.

"Know that the only thing that exists in the Game, is the present moment of the Now and it is here where you should focus all of your creation. For every moment in the Now represents an entirely new reality

created by you. Look carefully and you will see what we mean. You will see that your life is broken up into frames which make up your movie. Stand back far enough and you can see that it is all unfolding in the present moment of the Now. Whether you agree with it or not, everything in your life is unfolding simultaneously in the Game.

"Understand that though your life may appear to be a linear stream of pictures, there is so much more happening within each and every frame. This is where things can change quickly in your life. Look closely and you will see." Within seconds, I was drawn in so closely that I was standing on a frame the size of a football field. "Look all around you. What do you see?" Caleb asked, as an army of thinly sliced frames suddenly appeared, hovering in every direction. "Do these look familiar? They should, because they represent the same tracks we showed you a moment ago. Except that now, these tracks are veering off in a multitude of directions from simply one frame of your life.

"Each frame represents a portion of an event that is occurring in the Now. More importantly, each is independent of the other and as such they represent an entirely new reality. Do you understand how monumental changes in one's life can be achieved in a fraction of a second? Although they may only represent a portion of any one event, each frame can alter your reality in ways you have yet to imagine? In other words, put them together as you would a flip book and watch an event come to life. Stop the book

and you will see the story as a stream of independent pages. Do you understand the magnitude of what is being shown to you?"

The question was a bit rhetorical since Caleb did not wait for an answer. "The significance is that what you believe to be a moment in your reality is actually the culmination of millions of independent realities coming together to form one frame. Change your expression and you change which reality lays on top of the other. Change that reality and no matter how similar it may appear to be relative to your existing world, you have now changed your life forever. In fact, you have also changed your past to reflect what you are experiencing in the present.

"It is in the Now that everything can change and does. This is not some philosophical or esoteric concept to ponder over. For we are simply showing you the multi-dimensional nature of your universe. Step back again and see how everything is unfolding in the present moment of the Now. Know that these concepts you hold of the past and the future are only an illusion of the mind. For nothing can happen in the Game that does not happen in the Now.

"Remember that everything has its own energy frequency. Therefore, in order for you to experience a reality that matches your desires, you must first learn to control your vibration in the Now. Control your vibration and you will learn to control the Game. Control the Game and you will change your world immediately. The Game is designed to comply

with your dominant desires. It must, for it is a Universal Law!"

"But how do I control my vibration?" I asked, as I felt my mind ready to explode. I was pulled even further back as I could now see the entire graph again. "Do you see that vertical line?" Caleb asked. "It delineates what you know as your past and your future. The horizontal line delineates what you know as your state of beingness through emotion. Where they intersect is where you are at any given time in the present moment of the Now.

"The horizontal line, which measures time, is contingent on your thoughts. It is your thoughts that can transport you back and forth from your present moment. The vertical line is contingent on your feelings, for they can transport you up and down the graph based on the frequencies you are emoting. Anything below the horizontal line represents a slower, more negative frequency. Anything above it represents a faster, more positive frequency.

"There is a whole range of emotions you know as feelings. They are all based on two emotions – love or fear. What feeling you express is motivated by the thought you are having. Therefore, feelings are actually the expression of thought and emotion. It is imperative that you understand this for every feeling you have contains its own frequency you know as an expression.

"It is that frequency that is expressed as a language of the heart that only the Universe can understand. It is

that language, with that specific coding or expression, which ultimately influences the coding of the Divine DNA. Know that the Divine DNA is designed to match the coding you are expressing with whatever reality exists within the limitless possibilities of the universe. In other words, everything you believe to be your reality in the present moment of the Now is a direct result of your thoughts and emotions. The entire universe is wired to your consciousness, making you the master operator of the most sophisticated, computer program ever created."

"Does that mean I don't exist? That I'm just part of some computerized program that is being run by someone 'out there?'" I asked, somewhat distraught at the possibility that my life could be easily summed up using a sequence of zeros and ones. "No, you do exist," Caleb insisted. "However, you are missing the point. We are trying to explain how the Game works so that you can come to master its controls. That you are Consciousness experiencing yourself in every imaginable way through a human existence within a simulated game you call your life.

"You exist as physicality through the manifestation of your avatar whose neural system is part of a greater network that spans throughout the physical universe. As Consciousness, you control the Game by controlling the vibration you know as feelings. These feelings are the expression of your thoughts and emotions. Control your thoughts and emotions and you control the Game. Control it long enough and you render it obsolete!" (see Figs. 7.4 through 7.6).

Creation in the Present Moment of the Now

The Purpose of Thought, Emotion & Beingness

Figure 7.4

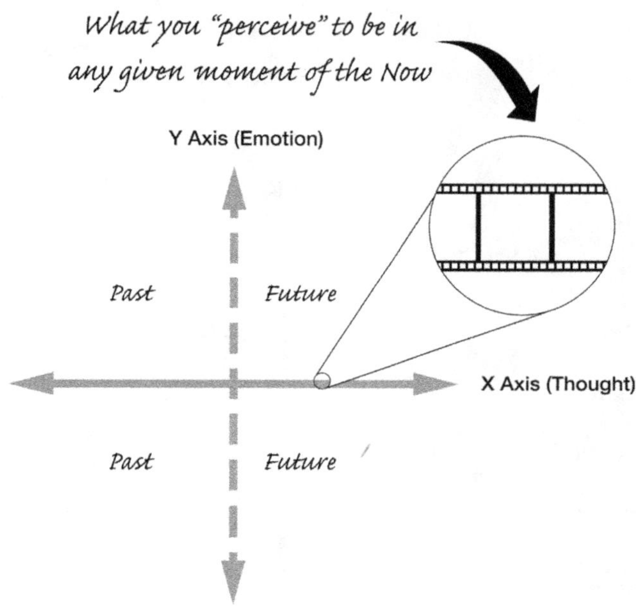

The Now in the 3rd Dimension

In the original dream state, we are led to believe that time is linear. A state of mind that even our Left Brain Consciousness finds difficult to rationalize. In this version of the Game, thought is "king" as only it can transport us back and forth from our present moment to relive the past. Worse yet, use our past to shape our future in the Now. In either case, robbing us of the only thing that matters when it comes to creating our reality – the present moment. Since thought has no true sense of beingness, it relies heavily on our physical senses to reaffirm that which already "is" rather than what "can be." The latter existing completely independent of the past. Forcing us to believe in a life that is linear in nature and created by forces somewhere *out there!* (Note: Emotions, represented by the y-axis, are viewed as irrelevant to the original dream state; thus, shown as a dotted line on the graph.)

Creation in the Present Moment of the Now

The Purpose of Thought, Emotion & Beingness

Figure 7.5

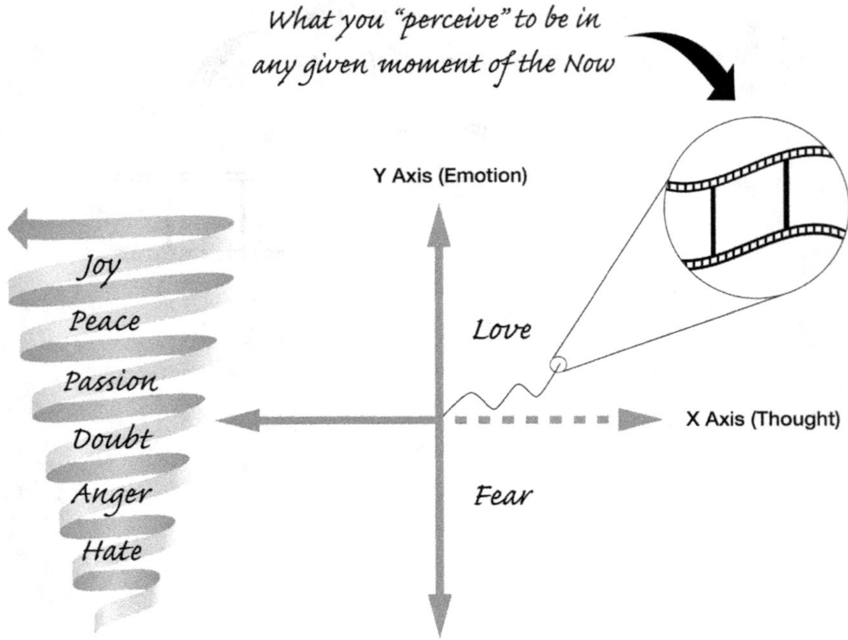

The Now in the 4th Dimension

In the new dream state, we are awakened to a belief that we are somehow much greater than our physical selves. A state of mind that runs contrary to our physical reality. One that is centered on the emotion of love rather than fear. It is here where we introduce emotion as an energy that can alter our sense of reality. Making life less linear by bringing forth into physicality what we desire from the metaphysical. Unbeknownst to us, our lives look more like a "roller coaster" ride when plotted on a graph. Feelings and desires, based on both thought and emotion, begin to dictate where we land in any moment of the Now. Know that when you come to understand this, and you will, you will begin to make "deliberate" changes to your life for the better.

Creation in the Present Moment of the Now

The Purpose of Thought, Emotion & Beingness

Figure 7.6

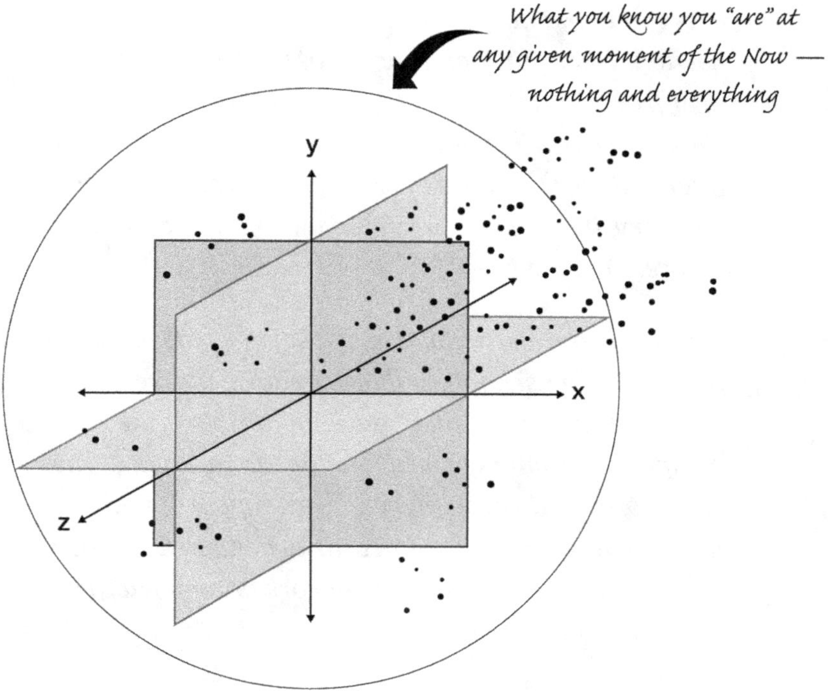

What you know you "are" at any given moment of the Now — nothing and everything

y

x

z

The Now in the 5th Dimension

In the awakened state of the 5th dimension, we are introduced to a heightened state of awareness we know as the God Consciousness (i.e., the z-axis). It is this state of beingness that enables us to transcend the perceived limitations that we are living any one specific moment at any time, rather than all moments, all the time. It is here that we will not only come to understand the multidimensionality of the Now, but we will also come to embody it. It is important to know that this level of consciousness is with us even in the lower frequencies of the 3rd dimension. It is the God Consciousness that gives us the perception of space because God Consciousness is everywhere, all the time. Therefore, "we" are everywhere, all the time. We just don't know it in the 3rd dimension.

"Wait a minute, say that again," I asked, as if to question what I had just heard loud and clear. "This is where you are at. It is time for you to end this game. You have all experienced yourselves in every imaginable way. The Game is simply no longer needed. Once you free yourself of the Game, you will also free yourself from all forms of the dream state. This process will not take very long. For it was not intended to take thousands of your years. On the contrary, it is happening right now and will end when you reclaim the rulership of this Truth.

"It is the only reason you chose to come here at this time. The schooling that humanity has received here on earth is complete. As with any class that has completed its coursework, it is time to graduate. The Game provided you with an endless supply of realities to achieve what you wanted to accomplish in your lesson plan. Humanity's coursework is complete. The Game is no longer needed."

"But how does one control their thoughts and emotions to complete the ascension that is required to end the Game?" I asked, a bit frazzled knowing that I was reaching the climax of our discussion. "Understand that you are already controlling the Game. There is nothing that the Game does without your consent. Through your Left Brain Consciousness, you have been controlling the Game all along. It simply hadn't occurred to you, because up until now you were unaware that the Game existed.

> *"To control the Game the way you desire, it must come from portions of your consciousness that have been dormant until now. Those areas are now awakening and with the help of your Attributes, they will continue to awaken and remain that way. You have everything you need to control your vibration. All that remains is for you to 'be still and know.'" And with that said, my transmission with Caleb was done.*

I remember crying after that particular Download. I knew that what Caleb had shared was the primary reason for why I was here. Why we were all here. That is, to help ease the labor pains of a world that was about to give birth to a new reality. Any thoughts I had harbored of a cruel and vindictive world disappeared. The battle I had waged internally for so long was coming to an end. I knew there was still work for me to do but I could finally see the light at the end of the tunnel.

It was time for me to finish my quest. The one that I had started many years ago and which was now leading me to the summit of a new reality. It was time for me to find that child, trapped deep within, that once ran freely in the meadow I knew as my innocence. The child that would help reunite me with my higher Self. And the only one that could help put an end to the Game, once and for all!

Chapter Eight

The Inner Child

There exists within us all a state of beingness so pure that any semblance of resistance vanishes in its presence. An awareness so thoughtful that it sees nothing other than the light of profound beauty. It knows the world to be nothing less than magical, because it is. Everything in this state of beingness has its place and purpose, for everything is God.

The beingness I speak of is that of the *Inner Child.* A frequency of light comparable to that of the higher Self that embodies everything we know ourselves to be. That is to say, as God we know ourselves to be peace, love, happiness, and spiritual freedom. We know this Truth as our "Core Beingness." A beingness we have spent our lives searching for only to realize it was never lost. The Inner Child is there to remind us of this Truth. It exists in a state of blissful innocence because in doing so it knows itself to "be" regardless of the egoic mind.

Growing up we are told to ignore that innocence. To run away from it as fast as we can into adulthood. To surrender ourselves to the egoic mind that is obsessed with controlling you and the operations of its outer reality. Keeping you focused on a world that already exists rather than the one you know inside to be. The one that is ready to come forth if only you knew of its existence. We chastise those that hold on to their innocence. Accusing them of being naïve or "out of touch" with reality. Never realizing the irony that lies within that statement.

Naivety and ignorance are the instruments of choice to our Inner Child. They allow the Inner Child to go beyond the trappings of the mind so that it can experience the Game for what it really is. "And what exactly is that?" you will ask. In simple terms, the Game is a playful, interactive tool there to inspire the Inner Child to remember who he or she has always been. The Inner Child knows itself to be the "key" by which to navigate through the complexities of the Game with little to no resistance. And why? Because resistance does not exist in the stillness that is the Inner Child.

In the dream state, duality was created with resistance in mind. It is the very nature of resistance that gives us purpose to seek out a deeper meaning in life. To know ourselves as God by knowing what we are not. And to question that dichotomy by resisting what we know is not our true nature. This was the purpose of the original dream state. And to that end, its purpose was served. The Inner Child was given a limited role in the dream state. To serve as a painful reminder of who we truly are but have since forgotten. Yet, another cruelty of the dream state.

The Inner Child holds no judgment as to the purpose of the dream state. To it, the dream state is simply a magical place to experience itself in a way it has never done before. It watches with curiosity as the circumstances of life unfold before it. It delights in what it sees and chooses not to give it any further meaning, for it knows no duality. To the Inner Child, it is simply observing from a place of stillness. Knowing that whatever is unfolding will soon pass if it does not serve to please the Inner Child. In other words, if what is being observed does nothing to align the Inner Child with its Core Beingness of peace, love, happiness and spiritual freedom, that energy will fade away.

The Core Beingness is embedded in every aspect of what you know of as physical reality. It contains a very unique sequence of codes that are embedded within the fabric of the Game itself. As God, you and only you have access to these codes. In fact, you have access to every code that exists. The Universe, as the Game, responds only to these codes. It is continuously expanding as each and every one of you provide it with more information that is unique to yourselves.

As our inner worlds expand, so does our physical reality. There is no separation that exists. It is simply the inhaling and exhaling of what we know God to be. Which is to say, the "Universal Mind" of which we are all a part of. We are all contributing to that expansion in ways that are unfathomable to the limited mind. And yet, to the Inner Child, it knows this to be simply a Game. Immersing itself deep within the Game until the two become indistinguishable. Leaving the Game to take its rightful place as a servant would to its master.

Realize the magnitude of what has just been said. The Inner Child only knows the coding sequence by which to create a reality aligned with its Core Beingness. Therefore, it enters the Game with a much higher frequency than what we are capable of achieving as prisoners of our social conditioning. Remember that the Game operates through coding we send to the Universe as energy frequencies we know as feelings. Change those feelings to a higher frequency and you change the sequential coding of the Divine DNA. Change the sequence and you change your world. But to know this is not enough. You must come to experience this Truth if you are to permanently awaken from the dream state.

As I have gotten older, I have come to rely on my Inner Child. To watch my world as it innocently unfolds before me. To let life simply be, or as Caleb would say, to merely "be still and know." This is probably the most difficult habit I have had to learn. For like you, I have learned to react to everything in my outer reality. I have played the role of victim very well. Reinforcing the truths of others that were fed to me at an early age. Therefore, to be the stillness and know my outer reality for the illusion that it is, has been absolutely excruciating to my ego and its sense of reality.

Nevertheless, my Inner Child has helped me to see beyond the chaos and clutter of my life. To free my mind to imagine the unimaginable relative to my future and its endless possibilities. To help me bring those possibilities into the Now so that they, along with the present moment, inspire me to live freely in my pursuit of peace, love, happiness and spiritual freedom.

My Inner Child has taught me to go beyond my physical senses to explore the metaphysical world that defines me as Spirit. It has given me the courage to take my faith to new heights. To soar way beyond hope or thinking, to places of knowing and understanding so that I might remember that which I have always been. To take a leap of faith into the unknown. To live life with the best of intentions while treating my world with love and compassion.

My Inner Child has become a doorway by which to travel through to my spiritual oasis. A portal enabling me to go deep within the serenity of my stillness. A place that exists in some far away dimension I call home. It is there that I have been blessed to be reunited with my spiritual family. Those who I came to know here on earth, as well as others who have been with me since before time. Without my Inner

Child and the innocence it maintains, it is unlikely that I would have achieved so much in so little time.

My Inner Child has brought me so much clarity. A state of lucid balance that comes from being in tune with its frequency and that of the higher Self. It has been my guide, my healer, in my quest to remember what I have always known but have forgotten. It has been my beacon whenever I have found myself wandering too far from my original course. My Inner Child knows no fear nor would it know how to create such an emotion. It lives in a state of perpetual harmony and bliss. It entered this world with me, and despite being set adrift into the dream state early in my adolescence, it has never left my side.

The light that shines from my Inner Child is brilliant and can be seen and felt throughout the universe. Since it only knows peace, love, happiness and spiritual freedom, my Inner Child goes about playfully interacting with the world. Speaking to it as if they were soulmates. Eternally connected by the etheric network of the Universal Mind. To my Inner Child, everything is Oneness. As such, it knows nothing of duality until it is taught to do so.

My Inner Child exemplifies the purest intentions of whatever we call God. Since it has no personal agenda, it believes the Game to be nothing more than a playful reflection of itself. It has an intrinsic understanding of the Game and delights in its magic. Viewing the Game as a means to an end where only the imaginative mind is allowed to enter and play. And as always, doing so in complete synchronicity with the rhythmic sounds and impulses of the Universe as it knows itself inseparable from Oneness.

> *"Find your Inner Child and you will know your Self," Caleb whispered, sensing my desire to break the code of my redundant behavior. A lesson I was struggling to comprehend. "The Inner Child is who you are and*

have always been. Find your Inner Child and you will come to know your inner Self," Caleb repeated.

"Know that the Inner Child is light. A light so pristine that it can alter your world in ways you have yet to imagine. But it is a light that you cannot see with your eyes, for it shines brightly in frequencies that are much higher than what you know in your physical reality. Therefore, you must go within to find your Child."

"Caleb, I am just starting to understand how to view my world inwardly. I don't know if I can find this Child," I answered, feeling somewhat uneasy and rather insecure about my capabilities. "There is nothing to search for," Caleb would quickly respond. "The Inner Child is not some place you need to spend a lifetime searching. It is a state of beingness which you have always been but have forgotten.

"The Inner Child is who you are and who you will always be. Quiet your mind and surrender to your imagination, for it is there that you will find your Inner Child once again." My mind went silent, as if someone had disconnected me from some imaginary outlet. There was darkness and silence everywhere. And yet, I could feel myself drifting deeper within. A light appeared in the distance. As it drew closer, a magnificent picture began to form.

"Caleb, why am I here again?" I asked, as I gazed at my meadow, captivated by its beauty. "This is your world," Caleb replied. "It is here where you will find your Inner Child and together you will come to

know your higher Self. It is here where you are free to create without resistance.

"As we have said before, many of you believe that such a place only exists after death, but that is simply not true. For what you call death is simply a state of beingness that exists in a higher frequency. Such beliefs are an illusion that you have created to keep yourself from remembering the Truth. Which is to say that everything in your physical reality is simply a simulation of the mind; created by you for you, to experience yourself as God through duality. A game that has served its purpose but is no longer needed in its present form.

"It is time to surrender to the Inner Child, for it will show you how to end the Game without resistance. In doing so, you will awaken from the dream state only to find that you never left home. That you have always been here as the higher Self waiting for your own return. Find the Inner Child and you will find your way back. Find your way back and you will remember that you are God."

I could feel that Caleb was drawing my attention to a tree that towered effortlessly over everything in the meadow that overlooked my world. There, nestled within its branches was an enormous treehouse that stood at least ten stories high. It was adorned with magnificent lights whose colors I had never seen before.

I wasted no time in going inside only to find that I wasn't alone. There in the corner sat a beautiful, curly-haired child no more than five or six years old. He had the rosiest of checks and cocoa brown eyes. I could tell that he was completely absorbed in his imagination. His eyes fixated on his toys as he went about talking freely to friends I could not see. "Oh my God, it's me! It's me, Caleb!" I shouted, as tears began to stream down my face.

"I've missed you so much," I said, as I ran to embrace my Inner Child. I was greeted with the warmest smile and the softest giggle as we hugged for what seemed like an eternity. Every wall of resistance came crashing down as I could feel that my Inner Child was activating a sense of beingness deep within me. Every cell in my body began to vibrate as if it were cleansing my soul of its impurities. It was the most liberating feeling of euphoria I had ever felt.

"Be still and know that you and your Inner Child have never been separated," Caleb began. "When you find yourself struggling to clear your mind or when your heart is heavy, go back to your Inner Child and let it take you to the stillness you know as your home. Hold that energy as long as you can and you will activate the serenity within your heart. Create from within that serenity and you will change your expression. Change your expression and you will master the Game and change your life forever."

I have made many trips back home since then. I have used that time to develop a greater appreciation for my Inner Child. To allow my Inner

Child to take me deep within my inner world. I have come to know my Inner Child as a means by which to express my higher Self. To use its innocence to bypass the chaos and clutter of my egoic mind. To find the peace, love, happiness and spiritual freedom I had been searching for my entire life.

My Inner Child has allowed me to go beyond the limitations of my present mind to simplify my understanding of Consciousness. I no longer view Caleb as somehow separate from my higher Self. To me, Caleb is a collective of many individual consciousness of which my Inner Child, along with my higher Self, are a part of. Therefore, we are all one and the same. Such awareness has given me a stronger sense of reassurance knowing that I have always been able to communicate with my higher Self. A friendship I had been longing for since I could remember.

I cannot tell you how liberating it has been to know that everything I have come to view as Consciousness is simply a different reflection of me. That it doesn't have to be as complicated as it sounds if I am willing to tap into my Inner Child. I know that there are many who cannot say the same. The idea of a relationship with one's inner Self is beyond their comprehension. Not to mention one that involves their Inner Child. They have surrendered to the social construct who has led them to believe that such efforts are fruitless, if not disturbing, to society as a whole.

If only they could come to understand that such thinking is simply an illusion of the mind. A thought that was cleverly added to the dream state to throw them off their scent. For the Inner Child offers a state of beingness consistent with who they are as God. To have left it unchecked would have rendered the original dream state obsolete. Know that it is the Inner Child that will lead you to your personal awakening. For you represent an assembly of spiritual beings known as the "Children" who have come to bring forth their light so that others may find their path back to the Truth.

"Caleb, can you tell me about the Children?" I asked. For some time now I had been thinking of these beautiful beings. I could feel them all around me. Occasionally being reminded of their innocence in the presence of a child. But I knew them as more than just children. I knew them to be of all ages. Beings of higher vibration that are here for a specific purpose. What exactly, I did not know.

"The Children are here to usher in humanity's transition into higher Consciousness," Caleb replied. "They are here bearing the light of the Child. A frequency of light that is set to trigger when you have reached a certain vibration. They have been coming here for quite some time but never more so than now. They are beings who have mastered this level of consciousness long ago, and who have come here to bear witness to what you know as the 'Awakening.'

"Each Child has chosen to play one of three specific roles. It is important to understand that no role is greater than the other. For all three are absolutely critical to the Awakening process. It is also important to understand that the Children are here to assist in the 'celebration' of what is to come. There is no judgement day or calamity that will be cast upon humanity as foretold by some. For this is a time to celebrate the birth of a new world order.

"The first group of Children are known as the 'Teachers.' Throughout the course of human history

there have been many such Teachers. You know them as some of the greatest and most inspiring philosophers, prophets and intellectual minds of your time. But there have been many, many more. Teachers that were known only to certain indigenous groups who have since disappeared into the shadows of the dream state.

"The Teachers came to plant the seeds of knowledge and Truth so that one day humanity could remember. Though the Truth has been twisted over the years, the spirit of what they left was never tainted. For they left the blueprints by which humanity would find its way back to its Inner Child. The benevolent Self you know as God.

"In recent decades, the Teachers have come in greater numbers. They have done so because it is time to raise the frequency of consciousness on your planet. For you as God have achieved everything you set out to experience in this earthly school you know of as life. Therefore, it is time for humanity to graduate. To ascend to a higher state of consciousness.

"In order to raise the frequency of an entire planet, these Children agreed to come into your world forgetting who they were. The trials and tribulations they would endure would have to be great to produce such inner expansion of the mind. In essence, they knew they would have to experience their own rebirth for the metaphysical reality of the new dream state to be created. Then and only then could they share such knowledge with others.

"These Children came carrying their own cross so others might not have to. They have waged their own inner wars in search of their true identity. Though they are here in the name of spiritual evolution, some have come to raise awareness in other areas of consciousness, such as racial, gender and sexual equality on your planet. Knowing that this would help humanity gradually expose itself to the light after living for so long in darkness.

"Many of these Children are viewed as outcasts in a world that expects conformity through its social programming. Though they have questioned their own sanity many times over, they are now realizing that in fact, it is society that is insane. For that reason, they are here to redefine the rules of the Game. To declare once and for all that humanity has no clothes; thus, stands naked to the Truth. Know that you are among these Children. That you came to pave the way for those that are now coming forth with their light."

"But I haven't done anything," I answered, somewhat surprised at my own response. "I feel I have had this 'calling' for years. That I have known the Truth all along but I have been afraid to do anything about it. It saddens me to know how I have wasted my life."

"Know that everything happens in perfect time and in perfect order," Caleb was swift to respond. "That what you have done up until now, however little you may think it is, has contributed to the inward expansion of Consciousness and the Awakening that is about to happen. Know that your days of contributing

are just beginning, and that your time to shine brightly is fast approaching.

"The next group of Children are known as the 'Healers.' The overwhelming majority of them began arriving toward the end of the last millennium. Those that came before, did so to be on the frontlines with the Teachers. Caring for them as they went through their own Awakening. Constantly at attention, holding the light for others so that all could come to remember.

"The Healers possess extraordinary psychic abilities that many on your planet will soon discover for themselves. The most prolific being the gift of empathy which enables them to absorb the physical and emotional discomfort of others. Doing so quite naturally in the name of unconditional love. Wanting nothing more than to restore the balance of peace, love, happiness, and spiritual freedom in the lives of those they touch.

"The Healers came into this world set to a higher frequency than the Teachers. Allowing them to have a more lucid experience with their outer reality. An experience that would enable them to be 'in' this world but not quite 'of' this world. In other words, enabling them to experience all that their physical world had to offer while maintaining a level of innocence relative to their interpretation of life.

"At times, these Children have been susceptible to the drama of their world. Often manifesting, in some fashion, the physical or mental conditions they were trying to alleviate. You have seen this

play out in the preadolescent years of the physical child. Notwithstanding, their abilities to absorb such energies do not go away with age. In fact, for some it becomes increasingly difficult to cope with these sensitivities and the negative energies being drawn to them.

"But things are changing. The Healers are now awakening to the Truth that they are here to do more than just lessen the pain and suffering of your planet. They are here to balance the frequencies of the Awakening so that humanity can slowly adapt to the light of the Inner Child. In other words, they are here to assist in cleansing humanity of its negative energy. For in the Awakening, the detoxification of the mind can be rather unbearable for those unable to handle the weight of their past.

"The last group of Children are known as the 'Guardians.' They represent a smaller group of beings that, up until recently, have rarely shown themselves in physicality. You know them as your Ascended Masters, Spiritual Guides, Divine Beings, Saints, Angels and Arch Angels. They have been with humanity since the beginning of time. Always there maintaining the greater balance between light and darkness.

"Those that have manifested into physicality have entered at a level of frequency above all others. They are here, however, not to heal but rather to position themselves strategically so that when the higher energies arrive, they are present to receive its light

and manage its transmission. A process designed to manage the gradual exchange of energy as your planet ascends into a higher state of consciousness.

"These Children know themselves to be different. Intrinsically, they view their world differently and spend very little time trying to understand why. They allow themselves to drift untroubled and undisturbed by the illusion of their social programming. However, as the Awakening approaches, these Children are gathering themselves inwardly as they heed the calling of their inner Voice.

"Though their original mandate was to avoid interfering directly with the spiritual evolution of humanity, their presence in physicality is needed now more than ever to manage the changes that lie ahead. For they will provide an additional layer of balance to your world as they reinforce the silence within the noise. A field of unconditional love and tranquility that has been carefully woven within the fabric of everything that exists.

"The Guardians have no interest in playing the meaningless game defined by the social construct. Rather, they are here to play the only Game that matters – the one that operates all of reality. To do so, they have come here to interact with all that is sentient on your planet. For all sentient beings are essential in defining and reinforcing the field. In essence, the Guardians are here to oversee and protect the birthing of the global Awakening and the proper disbursement of its light."

"Caleb, please tell me how the Game factors into the Awakening and the role of the Inner Child in ending the Game?" I asked, not wanting to interrupt but also sensing the timeliness of my question. I knew Caleb had answered this question before, but I still needed some assistance in connecting the dots. "The Game was originally designed to facilitate the physical reality of your desires," Caleb responded. "It is a holographic simulation designed to implement and achieve the goals set forth by all of you as God. Goals and desires to experience yourselves in every imaginable way through this human existence.

"Since the goals have all been achieved, the original dream state is no longer needed, nor is the Game as it currently exists. As such, the Children are here to facilitate the orderly transition of the Game as well. For as humanity awakens from the dream state, it will find itself in unfamiliar waters. Therefore, it is not that the Game will end right away, but rather that it will evolve into a playful tool by which all will come to remember and experience their Inner Child. A state of pure divinity you know yourself to 'be' as God.

"It is time now to merge the Inner Child with who you believe yourself to be in this physical reality. An assimilation of consciousness for which the Game was designed to handle. When that transition is over, so will your need for the Game. You have all experienced this metamorphosis many times in what you call your physical death. The time is fast approaching when such transition will no longer be necessary to experience this reunion of the mind.

> *"Can you see now why the state of beingness we call the Inner Child is critical to the Awakening? Why in time it will end the Game like any child would end any other game it has mastered? Humanity has chased its tail long enough. There is nothing more to experience on this earthly plain that has not already been experienced a million times over. It is time to bring forth Heaven on Earth. Your lessons are all complete. It is time to move on!" And with that said, my transmission with Caleb went silent.*

Caleb's message was so simple and yet so complicated. Simple because it made sense. Complicated because it defied everything I had been taught to believe. Complicated because I could also sense that my inner quest was coming to an end, though it wasn't clear to me exactly how or why. What I did know, however, was that I was finally feeling at peace with my spiritual beingness. That I had this wonderful friendship with my Inner Child for which I had Caleb to thank. Though I was still fighting the programming of my past, I was determined to follow my Inner Child. To take that leap of faith and follow the path least traveled.

I could sense that Caleb was urging me to take that leap. To defy all conventional wisdom that would advise against such foolish behavior. To see myself as something greater than I could ever have imagined. To take stock of my own self-worth, knowing that it alone was at the root of all my fears. To embrace my empathetic abilities and my calling to help humanity find its way back to the light.

My Inner Child was ready to assist me in taking back the controls of the Game. To help me navigate through the last vestiges of my inner Awakening. A rite of passage I would have to overcome if I were to help humanity do the same. A responsibility I willingly accepted, along with many others, before coming here in physicality. "But why now?" you might ask. That one is actually quite easy to answer. To assist humanity as it stands at the doorway of its own Awakening. An event so extraordinary that it will give birth to a new world in a universe that has yet to be created!

Chapter Nine

The Awakening

I want to take you to a magical world that exists outside of thought and emotion. Way beyond the illusion of our physical world and our five senses. A world where the analytical mind cannot enter, for it knows only duality. A state of beingness that does not exist here. In this world, you have no identification to the physical self. You know yourself as nothing and yet everything to all. By nothing, I mean you are Consciousness, and therefore you have no name. And since you have no name, you are free to be everything.

This world I speak of knows no death, no sickness, no sadness nor pain of any kind. There is no such thing as time and space. Gravity does not exist here nor does sound or light in the manner you have come to know them. More importantly, what you know as fear cannot exist here. "But why?" you might ask. Because fear is a fabrication of the mind. The analytical mind to be exact. A sophisticated illusion by which to keep you imprisoned, or shall I say, addicted to your physical reality.

There is no greater addiction than that of fear. For without the duality it represents, the Game and the dream state could not exist. You see, everything in your physical reality is predicated on the notion that you must never know your authentic Self. For to do so, would be comparable to knowing the ending of a good book before you start. Or, to play a game that you know you have already won. What joy would there be in that?

Great lengths were taken to disguise this illusion in the original dream state. Every imaginable form of contrast was created to draw our attention away from the Truth. A web of deception that would weave its way into your stream of consciousness before birth. Using your empathic abilities to innocently absorb these lower frequencies from your mother and other factors in your environment, while still in her womb. As if that were not enough, religions would instill within us an unspeakable burden of fear through our association with karmic debt and original sin. All but guaranteeing that we would come to know fear as a core essence of our beingness.

It is here that I will begin the story of our Awakening. For to awaken is to let go of our addiction to all fear. To see it as nothing more than the illusion that it is. I admit, this will be much easier said than done. For many of you will deny having such an addiction. "That is the most ridiculous thing I have ever heard!" you will say. "I hate my fears and want nothing to do with them. You don't know what the hell you're talking about!" And yet, in the same breath you will admit to living each moment as if it were in your past or some version of the future based on that past.

Since our social construct is programmed to instill fear, by default we are left craving the very thing we swore to fight against. Therefore, our past will lead to certain thoughts. Those thoughts will inspire fear-based intentions which are then emoted as energy signatures we know as feelings. Hence, leaving us to repeat our past over and over again until we are able to somehow break this vicious cycle.

What we fail to understand is that the process of emoting feelings creates a chemical addiction at the cellular level. An addiction that leads to the rewiring of neural networks and the resequencing of the DNA in our physical body. If this sounds familiar to you, it should. This is exactly what happens at the subatomic level of our holographic universe and the Game we are playing. This is what Caleb was trying to explain relative to the Divine DNA. And yet, the analytical mind will fight this Truth to the bitter end. I know because I am guilty of doing so myself.

The Truth is that humanity does not even know it has an addiction, much less that this addiction is keeping it from awakening into a higher state of consciousness. Therefore, to know nothing of this process is to be asleep in the original dream state. To say you have experienced some aspect of this Truth, but yet still identify yourself with the egoic mind, is to believe that you are awake within the lucidness of the new dream state. It is only when you come to see all reality from the perspective of Oneness that you will know yourself to be truly awake.

But what exactly does that mean? And how does one go about achieving Oneness so as to wake up from all forms of the dream state? Though I could feel that I was nearing the end of my quest, I simply could not find the answers to these and other questions that were plaguing my mind. It would take Caleb to remind me that the problem lies within the very approach I had chosen to take. That I was trying too hard to uncover these Truths with the analytical mind rather than from the perspective of the Right Brain Consciousness. A painful mistake I had made years before in my initial Awakening and one I was determined not to make again!

One morning, as I was waking up, I could hear Caleb's voice echoing in the distance. It had been some time since they had welcomed me with a morning mantra. But unlike some in the past, this one felt a little different. I could almost sense Caleb's compassion as if to acknowledge the heightened sensitivity of the topic that was about to be discussed.

"Caleb, what is it that you want me to know?" I asked. Caleb went silent but I could sense there was a significant Download on the horizon. "Let it be," Caleb would say softly as their mantra started up again. Like a child sitting curbside at a parade, I listened with unbridled enthusiasm as I waited for the next Download to begin.

"The end of your quest is near but there is still frustration," Caleb replied. "The frustration you feel is because you are still asleep in the lucidness of your dream state. No different than the dreams you once had as a child where you would awaken only to realize you were still asleep within a dream. In this case, you know yourself to be more and yet your association with the physical self has left you vulnerable to the subtle dualities and fears of the new dream state."

Caleb's news came as a shock to me. My first reaction was to think that they had mistaken me for someone else. Or that somehow I had woken up in yet another dream. Expecting neither to be the case, I quickly went into denial, though it didn't take much for Caleb to convince me otherwise. "To know you are in the dream state," Caleb continued, "is to realize how dependent you are on your physical reality. You say you are not 'of' your physical world, yet you do not show it by how you react to external events.

"To make matters worse, you are still using your mind to rationalize your inner quest. The very mind that led you astray in your initial Awakening. You must remember how to use your heart in coherence with your mind. For the heart is the bridge that connects you to who you are as God Consciousness. Take solace in knowing that this is all part of the Awakening process.

"We want to be very clear so that you can come to appreciate what is being conveyed. This will not only help you to correct your course of action, but also enable others to avoid making the same mistake. To begin with, the separation of mind and consciousness is simply an illusion. To be more exact, the mind is the analytical manifestation of consciousness. Therefore, there is no war to wage between the two because duality does not exist here.

"Clear the mind of its clutter and it will come to understand this powerful Truth. The mind will remember that everything, be it physical or metaphysical, resides within Consciousness. Therefore, since you are Consciousness, everything resides in you! It is imperative that you understand this. For the physical self is simply one expression of you as God existing within the many layers of your consciousness.

"Understand that there is nothing you need to achieve. This is yet another illusion created by the original dream state. In the higher states of awakened consciousness, you cannot achieve that which you already are. Therefore, only 'awareness' is needed to experience a full Awakening. This is not conjecture but rather, Universal Law."

"I am still having difficulty understanding," I interrupted, feeling frustrated at my inability to grasp what Caleb was saying. "Do you recall the analogy of being the actor, director and producer of your play?" Caleb asked, knowing full well that I would remember. "The only difference here is that in the world of Oneness, there is no need to climb out of any screen to manipulate your reality. "And why not?" you might ask. "Because you 'are' the screen. You 'are' reality. Everything exists inside of you!"

"But if I am all of these things, then I am everything!" I shouted out in my mind. "And if I am everything, then I am also the universe, which means I am the very Game I have been trying to control all along." My mind was racing uncontrollably as I could feel the neurons of my beingness coming together in a way they had never done before. A connectivity of consciousness between the physical body and the universe unimaginable to the rational mind.

"Close your eyes and see yourself as nothing going beyond thought and emotion. Stand there in the stillness knowing that you are the stillness and tell us what you feel?" It didn't take long before I could

sense a wave of energy all around me. As I paused to observe this phenomenon, I began to realize that its source was coming from deep within me. That I was both the stillness and the movement of this poetic dance.

There was no beginning nor end to my existence. Not only was I finally understanding the concept of Oneness, but I was also experiencing it as well. A spiritual breakthrough that was benefiting more than just me. For I could feel my Oneness penetrating every aspect of my physical reality. A marriage between two worlds that had been strictly forbidden for the sole purpose of keeping the dream state alive.

"The more you remain in this space the more you will come to remember," Caleb added. "The authentic Self that is you will become clear as the walls of duality come crashing down once and for all. The light of the Inner Child will enter in softly to celebrate the reunion of these two worlds. Surrender to the Truth and you will be set free.

"The shackles of fear that once held you prisoner within your mind will be removed. You will no longer see your physical reality as separate from who you are as God. There will be nothing left to fear other than fear itself. And though this will be quite obvious to you, the addiction to fear will be unlike any other. This is the last hurdle you must overcome. For the dream state and the chaos it has created through fear are nothing but illusions of the mind.

"Does this make sense to you?" Caleb asked, waiting for my approval before continuing. "Fear is your greatest addiction. It is the chemical by which you justify your allegiance to your physical reality. Your body and that of your physical universe crave this chemical despite the fact that you despise its existence. You treat fear as though it is separate from you and therefore beyond your control. As such, you create a world that reinforces the pathological behaviors that keep your fears alive.

"Knowing what we have shown you now, can you see the perverseness of such behavior? Imagine if you were to stand in front of a mirror only to scream in horror at the person staring back at you. To be terrified of your own reflection in the water or by your own shadow. That is what the illusion of fear has caused you to do in the dream state.

"The time has come for you to remember, for the light of the new Awakening is fast approaching. An Awakening that will have global ramifications for humanity. No longer will you be blinded by the veil of ignorance, for it is time that the Children remember who they are and why they came here. To bear witness to the Truth, and to hold and balance the light as its frequencies enter into this physical reality.

"It is time to cleanse yourself of the lower frequencies you came here to experience so that you, along with many others, can teach humanity how to find its way back to the light. It is time for you to let all things be in your outer world. To realize that everything you

are experiencing in your outer reality is simply an illusion. An illusion driven by the chemical imbalance of fear that feeds your addiction. It is time to enter into the stillness and let go of your fears. It is time to wake up once and for all!"

Caleb was right. It was fear that was holding me back from reuniting with my higher Self. I had reached a point in my quest where I was becoming fully aware of my divinity. Yet, I could not let go of my attachment to physicality. I could not let go because of my addiction to fear. "What if I was wrong?" I would ask with the analytical mind. "What if everything I had come to believe through Caleb was simply a delusional state that I had somehow walked into after all these years? And even if it were true, what if I wasn't worthy of such greatness? Or worse yet, what if I would fail in accomplishing what I came here to do?"

On my 54th birthday, I made up my mind that it was time to wake up. That it was time to answer these questions by walking into the unknown. To face my fears, not with aggression, but rather with love and compassion. Understanding that these states of beingness were here to show me a new, more profound way in which to experience myself as God. It was time for me to surrender what was left of my physical self to the Oneness with all. Though there would be much cleansing to be had, I knew that this was my way out. That this experience would break my addiction to fear and restore a greater sense of coherence back into my life.

With Caleb's support, I would use my meditations to go deep within the stillness of my silence. It was there that I would begin the healing process between the mind, heart and soul. To chip away at the clutter that I had been collecting all these years from my empathic abilities. To restore the brilliance of my Inner Child so that I could receive its light forever. I was finally standing on the shores of my serenity, looking out at an ocean of infinite possibilities.

As the walls of my prison came crashing down, I began to detect a much greater frequency. An energy of light whose impact on humanity would dwarf that of its predecessor from a decade ago. I had felt this energy before and knew that it was the Awakening Caleb had been alluding to in our talks. If I had any reservations about turning back, they had all but been destroyed by what I was sensing on the horizon. It was time not just for me to wake up, but for humanity to do so as well.

> *"Caleb, the Awakening is coming isn't it?" I asked, knowing all too well that something was about to happen. I remember having a similar feeling just before my first Awakening. Back then, I wasn't ready for the Downloads that would follow. To be honest, I wasn't too sure I was ready for them now. Despite my reservations, they were simply too beautiful to be ignored. For these were visions of a world that did not exist in this physical reality.*
>
> *"Do not be afraid," Caleb would answer, sensing my discomfort. "There is nothing that you need to revisit. Certainly, nothing with the analytical mind. For what you are seeing is Truth. Know that these visions are being revealed to you through a frequency that resonates with your Inner Child. A frequency that was not readily accessible to you until now.*
>
> *"Clear your mind and you will come to know that the Awakening you see is meant to be celebrated – not feared. That humanity has achieved everything it came here to experience. There are no more lessons*

to remember. The school you have come to know as this earthly plain is complete. It is time for this class of humanity to graduate.

"To fully appreciate the Awakening, one must first understand the transformational process each being must go through in their quest to be reunited with their higher Self. To begin with, this is but one of an infinite number of dimensions by which to experience yourself as God. Many of these platforms contain some aspect of duality, for without contrast one cannot appreciate the enormity of one's beingness.

"This earthly plain is considered to be among the most challenging of them all. Therefore, those that graduate are no longer required to go back and experience any platform containing the lower frequencies of consciousness. Notwithstanding, at one point or another you have all experienced many of these platforms. Often times experiencing them simultaneously. Hence, why you are known as multi-dimensional beings.

"In a universe that reflects itself in every imaginable way, is it any wonder that you have created virtual reality games on this earthly platform that mirror, albeit in a very simplistic manner, the Game you are playing as God? And look where you are now in your technological endeavors. You are at the very precipice of creating your own games that allow you to be the actual avatar!

"The Awakening is simply the acknowledgement that you have mastered the 'real' Game. That playing the

Game of duality has become so effortless that it and you are inseparable as Oneness. Therefore, there is no need to re-create in physicality what you as humanity have done as Consciousness. It is time to ascend into a higher state of beingness where other Games await. You know this process all too well for you have been through it many times before."

"Caleb, you use the word 'class' to describe humanity. Were there many before us?" I asked, utterly engrossed by Caleb's story as one would be sitting around a campfire at night. "There have been many before you," Caleb would reply. "There have been classes coming to this school for hundreds of thousands of your years. There are many others who have gone through a similar process in other schools, in countless dimensions, since before time itself.

"Each class evolving similarly to yours. At some point, frequencies rise, the Game is mastered and the class moves on to other Games in higher states of consciousness. In other words, humanity as divinity moves on to other worlds in other universes yet to be created. Many of your traditions know this higher state of beingness as heaven, nirvana, Zion, Jannah and more. In all instances, this realm cannot be crossed until death. Know that when the Awakening is complete, there will be no need for death. For you will know yourself to be greater than the body.

"As humanity awakens, it will remember these and many other Truths. And like you, humanity will have to determine whether to believe them or not. This is

the final rite of passage into the ascended levels of consciousness. Therefore, each being will be required to apply what they have experienced on this earthly plain within the context of the new dream state. A state of beingness they have never known before.

"For this will be the indicator by which they will know whether or not they have mastered the Game. Whether or not they have gone far enough within themselves to differentiate what is real and what is simply an illusion of the analytical mind. The vast majority will graduate and ascend to a higher state of consciousness. Those that do not will stay back to join the incoming class of divinity as they prepare to experience some form of human existence.

"Know that to stay back is not a form of punishment. There is no 'day of reckoning' like many of you have been taught to believe. There is no 'hell' nor is there this thing you call a 'devil' to reign over them. Those who remain will do so because they simply were unable to step into the unknown. To take that last leap of faith into the light. That being said, many of these beings will go on to become the next generation of Ascended Masters, Spiritual Guides, Divine Beings, Angels and Arch Angels.

"Regardless of their circumstances, those that remain will be tasked with creating and preserving the time capsules by which the next class will come to remember the previous civilization. But these capsules will serve an even greater purpose. For they will be discovered in the years leading up to each great

Awakening. Providing clues and cryptic messages intended to lead the next class back to the light. This is exactly what previous civilizations have done and why there are so many capsules being discovered at this time.

"Know that by time capsules, we are not referring to some metal contraption containing fragments of your civilization to be buried or shot out into space. We are referring to the energetic frequencies or signatures that will be embedded into the holographic programming of the next Game. Frequencies that will manifest themselves as clues and mysteries throughout the biological and metaphysical sequencing of the universal DNA.

"Look closely and you will see that such discoveries are now occurring at a spectacular rate. Rest assured that this is not a coincidence. The mysteries that are being uncovered at both the sub-atomic and atomic levels of your physical reality are staggering. Each day, there are discoveries happening that are raising more questions than answers relative to your current belief systems.

"The new sciences of your day are probing deep within the metaphysical world, only to find incredible correlations between Consciousness and your physical reality. Likewise, there have been remarkable discoveries in the field of mathematics relative to its role in how nature operates. Or in the similarities found between the binary coding system of your

computer language and how the universe functions as a whole.

"Archeological discoveries are now challenging the very construct by which humanity has used to explain its existence on your planet. There are discoveries being made all over your planet of civilizations that existed way before recorded time. But not just any civilization, these were extraordinarily-advanced societies comparable to what exists today, if not greater!

"There are even signs from the heavens in what you call crop circles and geoglyphs that appear all over your planet. Or the pyramids that are now coming to life, showing electromagnetic properties capable of transmitting energy similar to how your body operates. Or the steady growth of Teachers that are now communicating with Consciousness or ET beings from other dimensions in time.

"Everywhere you turn, there is increasing evidence pointing you back to the Truth. Telling you the same story regarding your authentic Self. The vast majority of this evidence having been discovered in recent years. These are all examples of what we mean by a time capsule whose energetic signatures are set to trigger when humanity reaches a certain level of frequency in its spiritual evolution."

"Caleb, can you please explain the purpose behind the next Awakening?" I asked, wanting reassurance that I was interpreting my Downloads or visions correctly. For I knew humanity had undergone a

similar Awakening back around 2010. "They are all one in the same," Caleb answered, having read my mind. "In other words, they are all part of the same process. Know that each Awakening has a specific function.

"Before we explain these functions, it is important to remind you that the Awakening has more to do with energy frequencies and the inner quest than anything you might experience in your outer reality. That being said, these events are not mutually exclusive. We are simply stating that if your expectations are based solely on what 'is' relative to your outer reality, then you will misconstrue the entire process.

"The Awakening is about remembering who you are. Knowing that you have never left the inner world you know as Consciousness. As such, the inner quest becomes much more relevant than the outer journey. That to focus on the latter is to remain asleep in the dream state. Measuring your life based on what has or has not changed in your outer reality. Never realizing that the act of doing so is what is keeping you from experiencing the very things that you desire.

"There are four stages of the Awakening that all must go through to complete their inner quest. We have alluded to these in various ways in the past, but it is now imperative that you understand them relative to what is happening in your world. The first is called the 'Intuitive Stage.' This stage is characterized by the subtle awareness that life doesn't seem to be adding

up in your physical reality. That something is inherently wrong or off with the outer world you inherited.

"In this stage, you are completely asleep, but yet more intuitive in nature. You acknowledge your inner Voice though no relationship evolves. Your identity is still with the rational mind and the physical self, but you find yourself having difficulty balancing your passions with what you rationalize as practical or common sense. The struggle between what you perceive to be real as conditioned by the social construct and what you know to be real in the experiential world, has left you questioning your purpose in life.

"Nevertheless, the seed of knowledge has been planted and before long, inquiry slowly gives rise to awareness which allows your vibrational set points to rise. The veil that once kept you hidden from your Inner Child begins to lift, revealing the subtle Truths of who you are and the real purpose for why you are here. Truths that cannot be rationalized by anyone or anything 'out there,' no matter how hard you try.

"The second stage of the Awakening is known as the 'Awareness Stage.' Though you are still asleep, you are now fully aware that you are doing so. Your allegiance to the social construct is weakening as you recognize the possibility that the world you inherited may very well be an illusion. But whose illusion and for what specific purpose remains unknown. For now, you are content in believing that the illusion has been fabricated by someone or something 'out there.'

"Despite what you know, you continue to identify with the rational mind and the outer world. Nevertheless, your inner Voice is relentless in reminding you of your authentic Self. Pushing you deeper into the realms of the Inner Child. Causing you to reflect on what was once pure in your beingness. Knowing that you will rationalize its intentions as a call for freedom between you and the rest of the world.

"So much is revealed to you in this stage but it takes time and patience before it will all make sense. For this aspect of the Awakening cannot be rushed, shortened or simplified in any manner. There is a spiritual purpose for why you came and thus, the experience cannot be cheated. You are intuitively aware of this Truth but are becoming inpatient. Craving answers without wanting to look inward for direction. Eventually, you embark on your inner quest and are greeted by an abundance of Truths that dramatically alter your perspective of both your inner and outer realities.

"Your epiphanies are short-lived as your dependency on your physical reality prevents you from fully embracing your inner world. Nevertheless, your intellectual awareness of the Truth leads you to believe that you have found the secret to all that you desire. When in actuality, you are simply reinforcing the illusion of the old dream state that wants you to remain within the walls of the analytical mind. Creating within the Game an experience where you are stuck between two worlds. Uncertain as to which one to pledge your allegiance to.

"The third stage of the Awakening is known as the 'Delusional Stage.' In this stage, you are still asleep but now believe you have awakened. You have accepted the belief that somehow you have escaped the prison of the dream state through the intellectual and spiritual awareness you have acquired along the way. Unaware that the dream state has you firmly in its grasp. Nevertheless, you are like a sponge soaking up all that you can in pursuit of the Truth.

"You dive deeper and deeper into your inner world to learn more as to who you are and your purpose for being here. You identify yourself as Consciousness but cannot let go of your attachment to the rational mind and physical self. As hard as you try to achieve enlightenment or to experience the life of your dreams, you simply cannot bridge the great divide between what you know is true and what is perceived to be real in your physical world.

"Eventually, you come face-to-face with the harsh reality that you are still asleep. A spell that cannot be broken until you have abandoned your addiction to fear. Your rite of passage into the ascended levels of consciousness depends upon your willingness to let go of everything you know in your physical world. To take the final leap of faith into the unknown. To go way beyond the intellectual mind in order to 'be' that which you already are.

"In the end, your experiential world becomes far more important to you than its analytical counterpart. Your desire for Oneness and a greater relationship

with both your inner Voice and Child takes precedent over matters of the mind. Spiritually, you are growing inwardly by leaps and bounds. The heart is now in control of the experiential mind as you begin to transition into the realm of God Consciousness.

"The last stage of the Awakening is known as the 'Ascended Stage.' In this stage, you have freed yourself from your physical addictions. Though you may enter having doubts or fears, they are insufficient in holding you back. You no longer identify with the physical self nor do you believe that you are occupying the same space with your rational mind. The walls of duality have been destroyed and you are free to remember that you have always been pure consciousness.

"The Game and all forms of the dream state have been rendered obsolete. All lessons have been learned and the rite of passage to graduate has been completed. The Inner Child is the state of beingness within which you now exist. There is symmetry in everything that you are and observe. You and your impulses are felt by Gaia and throughout the universe as you become fully aware of your Oneness with all.

"As a class, you are now ready to ascend into these greater states of consciousness whenever you desire. For the 3rd, 4th and 5th dimensions are but steps in a winding staircase that will take you home again. In the decade to follow, the world will come to know of the Ascension. Know that if you are a Teacher, it is your job to remind humanity that the Ascension we speak of is that of the mind knowing itself as Consciousness.

It is the reunion of you with your higher Self. The transformation of the physical into the metaphysical. The rebirth of who you have always been as God.

"The global Awakening that you are seeing through your visions represents the physical and metaphysical union of this transformation. In other words, as Consciousness experiencing itself in physicality, you are programmed with energy signatures you know as frequency codes. Some codes are specific to you, while others are embedded in the DNA sequencing of humanity.

"As frequencies rise beyond certain levels, these codes are activated to trigger a global Awakening. The intent is to initiate a gradual activation or Awakening while recognizing the fragile state of the collective mind. That is not to say that a global Awakening is needed to trigger these signatures. Throughout history, there have been many instances where individuals or groups of various sizes were able to do so without such an occurrence.

"One need only to look to your Ascended Masters to illustrate the point of an individual Awakening. Similarly, there are many examples of smaller civilizations that ascended out of your physical reality. Some leaving entire cities intact for humanity to speculate as to what might have happened. Never considering the possibility that a mass Ascension had occurred.

"The first global Awakening occurred between the years 2009 and 2012. By that we mean, the vast

majority of those whose codes were expected to be activated, were awakened at that particular time. However, there were others that would awaken in subsequent years due to the resonate energies of the Awakening. Regardless of its timing, the intent was to raise the energy frequencies on your planet to match that of the Inner Child.

"It would take the collective effort of all who heard the call of their inner Voice to bring forth that light. To raise frequencies high enough that time capsules all over your planet would slowly be activated. Capsules that would further inspire humanity to seek out the Truth. Many Teachers would awaken during this period to share their stories and to help others begin their quest in search of their higher Self.

"All told, millions on your planet would come to feel the effects of the first Awakening, but few would fully awaken. Among these would be a small army of Healers. A group of Children that came to hold the light while bringing balance to a world struggling to maintain some semblance of civility. A state of disarray caused by the expulsion of negative energy at that time. For all intents and purposes, the first Awakening is now complete.

"The second Awakening is to occur at the end of this year, 2019, and will last approximately three years. Like its predecessor, the vast majority whose codes are meant to be activated, will awaken during this time. Know that the intensity and scope of this global Awakening will be significantly greater than

its predecessor. For the intent of this Awakening is to touch many more lives with the specific goal of waking them all.

"During this period, energy frequencies will spike causing Gaia herself to awaken. A mass expulsion of negative energy will occur on your planet as Gaia prepares to receive the light of the Child. Vortices will spawn throughout your planet igniting a network of superconductors capable of regulating the tremendous amount of electromagnetic flow of light as it enters this time-space reality. It is here where structures like your pyramids will come into play. For they number well into the thousands and are strategically aligned to transmit the light to all corners of your world.

"Discoveries of time capsules will reach epidemic proportions leaving humanity thirsty for the Truth. The Science of Consciousness will weave its way into the very fabric of your social construct. Introducing metaphysical elements that have never been seen before. Though humanity knows very little of this science, all of that is about to change. For as energy frequencies rise, so will your access into the metaphysical world of the God Consciousness.

"In the second Awakening, humanity will witness the proliferation of peace, love, happiness and spiritual freedom. As such, the lower frequencies of deception that were once needed to sustain the original dream state will fade away making it difficult for the Truth to remain silent. No longer will you be guided by fear but rather by a growing desire to pursue your passion

and purpose in life. The calling to prepare humanity for its Ascension will supersede all other priorities.

"This will be a time of great planning. For this class of humanity is quickly approaching the shores of an unprecedented Awakening. Everything that will happen in the second Awakening is but a prelude to the third and final one. A dress rehearsal, if you will, for the rite of passage and the graduation or Ascension that will ensue. A production that has been thousands of years in the making.

"In the decade that will follow, tens of millions on your planet will come to feel the harsh but necessary effects of the second Awakening, many of whom will experience a full Awakening. Among these will be the Teachers, Healers and Guardians who came here to assist in the birthing of a new world order. For all intents and purposes, the second Awakening is now upon you – ready to make landfall!

"We know of your visions. We know that you have seen the arrival of a celestial portal that swirls over your skies and now stands at humanity's doorstep. This portal will arrive a few months before your Winter Solstice in the Northern Hemisphere. It is the portal of the Inner Child which brings with it the light energies or frequency signatures of the Ascension process.

"This is the energy that will help humanity remember who it is. There is nothing that you must do to receive it other than to 'be still and know' that all of this is being done by you for you. Listen to your inner Voice and let yourself be guided into the stillness of your

Inner Child. There you will come to know the Truth that you are all Gods. That this has been nothing more than a game that has allowed you to experience yourself through contrast.

"The third and last global Awakening will occur at the end of 2029 and will last for one generation. This is the Awakening that all of you came to experience. The graduation of humanity who will awaken to its authentic Self. Whereas the previous two Awakenings were designed to set the preparations in motion, the focus will now turn to humanity itself and its ability to transition into the higher states of consciousness that await.

"By all accounts, this is not meant to be a tortuous process. However, the trials and tribulations of accepting oneself as divinity will vary by individual and as such, will be fraught with fear and denial. Nevertheless, all efforts will be made to guide humanity into the light. For instance, spiritual beings will be given ample opportunity to ascend during this period as they will be allowed to incarnate into multiple lives. Ultimately, the decision to ascend or not will be left to each individual being, for that is the true nature of free will.

"In the final Awakening, many of the paradigms that have ruled over humanity will fall by the wayside, if they haven't already. Those that remain will be flipped right-side up again. Humanity's non-physical senses will rise to the surface as it welcomes the reunion of the God Consciousness within and around the

physical body. Though there will be many miraculous events prior to this Awakening, the period that will follow will come to be known as the 'Age of Miracles.' The period preceding what some have called 'The Golden Age.'

"As millions awaken, they will be inspired to share their visions with one another. A global collaboration of initiatives will ensue whereby the quietest and most isolated among you will make the greatest contributions to humanity. Social, along with other causes of all shapes and sizes, will be revisited with an entirely new perspective on how they should be resolved. At its root will be humanity's awareness that anything is possible, for everything is simply energy manifesting itself as some form of you based on your desires. Here are but a few examples:

"Medicine as you know it today will cease to exist. A new discipline will rise from its ashes whose foundation will be based upon the shifting and amplification of energy frequencies to heal the body. Therefore, giving credence to a global model of self-healing whose technologies and treatments will be non-invasive and non-destructive to the body, mind and soul. A complete departure of what exists today within the walls of your antiquated system of health care.

"Education will give way to a new discipline of 'remembering' that is 'experiential' in nature so that all are reminded of the Truth that lies within. As such, 'know'-ledge, wisdom and experiences will be shared

with one another for the betterment of Oneness in your world. A principle so vital that its absence in any model would deem that model to be obsolete in the world to come.

"Science as you know it will experience a renaissance unlike anything that could have been conceived in your current reality. Many of your disciplines will meld together and new ones will be born from ideas that have no earthly concept to you today. As humanity moves beyond the 5th dimension, concepts such as time, space, and gravity will cease to exist in the manner that you know them now.

"We ask that you take a moment to resonate with what is being said, for these paradigms are among the most powerful illusions created by the dream state. Though conceptually powerful as they may be in your current reality, there will be no reason for their existence in the world to come – NONE! We will use time to illustrate this simple point.

> *"Time was created as a means by which to introduce the illusion of structure and control in your lives. It operates under the laws of linearity created by the Left Brain Consciousness. Consequently, it has no relevance in the world to come, for that world will be based on the core principles of the Now and the energy signatures within which the universe operates.*
>
> *"Its very foundation will be breached once humanity comes to understand that*

> *in the Now there is no linearity, but rather dimensionality to its existence. In other words, one's ability to travel through this illusion of time is not a linear path, but rather a multi-dimensional path. For what you know as the past and the future exist concurrently in other dimensions of the Now. Dimensions that can be reached immediately through the use of energy signatures. And yes, such travel is possible even in your time-space reality!*

"As humanity transitions into the Ascension, the two worlds of the Awakening will split apart. Those that are not ready to receive the light will remain in the lower frequencies of this universe as we have already discussed. Those that ascend will be reacquainted with not only their higher Self, but also with friends and loved ones that have since passed into the spiritual realms of consciousness. For aging and death will have no significance in the higher frequencies or dimensions of consciousness where the body will go through its own lucid transformation.

"Know that there are many who exist in your physical reality that simply are not real. They are known as the 'Ghost People' and are part of the digital programming you know as the Game. We bring this to your attention because you will run into them throughout your Awakening. Know that they will not be sympathetic to your cause. For they are here to challenge humanity's resolve as it goes through its

rite of passage. Therefore, they will not be among those who will ultimately awaken.

"In addition, there are some that will ascend but will choose to come back in the early years of the new humanity. They will do so to help guide the new humanity through its infancy. No different than what other previous classes did for this group that is now graduating. One need only look at the walls of many of your ancient civilizations to see images or stories of these beings. Beings with elongated heads that towered over their human counterparts. Many of your ancient cultures and civilizations refer to them as the 'Star People' or 'Star Children.'

"Lastly, there are some of you that will inquire as to the duration of these earthly periods. Though it may vary from class to class, the earth experience typically ranges six to ten thousand of your years. Like any other school, the core curriculum will always be modified to ensure that each incoming class has a unique experience. Consequently, a whole new class will experience itself as God through a human existence. A process of expansion that goes on forever.

"Can you understand why there are so many coming here, right now, to assist humanity in its Awakening? To help give birth, not just to a new world, but to a new universe as well. For this is a time of celebration. A time where God as Source is experiencing the expansion of itself in unfathomable ways. The second Awakening will soon be upon you. Rejoice in its

arrival, for the world you know is about to go through a seismic change!"

I sat in my chair in complete silence. There was simply nothing more to do or say. Nothing more because it all made sense. My quest had taken me to the shores of my new reality. A huge part of my voyage was over. What laid ahead was the very thing I came here to experience. And though I could feel the grip of my egoic mind as it held on to me for dear life, I knew I had passed the point of no return. I had walked into the unknown only to find that the veil of darkness I had feared was simply my ignorance of the Truth.

A few days after my 54th birthday, my visions began to intensify. No longer were they limited to my dreams, for the portal Caleb spoke of was now visible to me in my awakened state. Swirling high above like a typhoon ready to make landfall. Its luminous clouds glistened with sparkling colors I had never seen before. Everywhere I looked there were signs of electrical activity as flashes of lightning raged in places deep within. And yet, at its core, there was this breathtaking silence. A quietness that spoke to my heart as if to assure me that all would be well.

One night, I dreamt that a beautiful sound was coming from within its silence. As I drew closer, I realized that I had drifted far from my earthly existence. Earth as I knew it was somewhere hidden among the stars. And yet, I could care less how I got to be in front of this magnificent portal. All I knew was that it was speaking to me in a language only my heart could understand. Calling me home to a place I have always known but had long since forgotten. As I looked down, I noticed that I had my book in one hand. Without hesitation, I threw the book into its abyss and within seconds, it triggered a light show unlike anything I had ever seen before. It was as though this action had somehow caused the universe to come back "online."

I knew right then and there why this book was meant to be written. I knew that no matter who read this book, tens of millions who didn't would still feel its effects. That encoded within it, were universal signatures that would help ignite the Awakening that was about to begin in earnest. As if somehow this book held the codes by which the eye of this magnificent portal would open and allow for the Inner Child to come rushing out. As I watched in absolute amazement, it occurred to me that I had reached the summit of my inner quest. That it was time for me to answer my spiritual calling. To surrender to my Inner Child and become the Teacher of the sacred Truth I knew I was meant to be!

Chapter Ten

The Calling

In writing this book, it was my desire to share the Truths within the context of my life. Hoping that one day humanity would not repeat the mistakes I made. That in the process of self-actualization, humanity might come to remember its authentic Self without the trials and tribulations I encountered. By sharing my story, it was my hope to inspire humanity to seek out its calling. That undeniable Voice that has been guiding it since birth.

To some, my story will seem bizarre and somewhat difficult to take seriously. Honestly, I wouldn't blame anyone for feeling this way since I have spent most of my life viewing it that way as well. And yet, despite all my cynicism and denial, the Voice within me never wavered. Calling me, time and time again, to remember and understand the true meaning of my life. A purpose that would become clear to me shortly after my first Awakening. A sense of knowing that I came here, along with many others, to help humanity remember its path back to the light. To help reunite it with something much greater than itself.

To define a "calling" is to describe it as an energy signature embedded deep within our DNA. Ready to remind us of our true identity and the purpose for which we came here. In the world of computer science, I guess you would call that a software program. Another way to look at it would be to call it a time capsule. An implant of some kind meant to be fully activated when our energy frequencies had reached a certain level of beingness.

Regardless of how you interpret them, one thing is for certain, the callings have a profound meaning relative to what is happening right now. But not necessarily for the reasons you might think. Yes, one can make a rather strong argument that the callings are happening because of our reckless abandonment. However, given what I have been shown, the real turmoil lies within each and every one of us. If only we could see ourselves for who we really are, we would wipe away the pain and suffering on this planet in a blink of an eye.

At this particular moment in human history, there is a tremendous calling happening all over the world. In the decades to come, millions upon millions will be called to remember a specific Truth. "And what is that?" you will ask. That we are so much more than what we have been taught to believe. That something deep within is calling us to greatness. Whether we choose to answer that call is entirely up to each and every one of us.

Know that if you are reading this book, it is YOUR calling that has brought you here. That no matter how convenient it may seem to discard your purpose for the sake of complacency, you did not come here for that reason. For your involvement is critical and unique, not only to you, but to everyone and everything that makes up your universe. For without your contributions, the path to humanity's Awakening will be fraught with difficulty. So then, what exactly is your calling? What extraordinary circumstances led you to read this book at this precise moment in your life, not to mention at this precise time in human history? And what, if anything, do you intend to do about it?

These are questions that only you can answer. Though it is safe to say that the answers you seek lie deep within your inner quest. A voyage into the unknown few of you care to make. As such, many of you will say that you are not ready to do the unthinkable, but I assure you that you are. For it is only when you do the unthinkable that the Truth will reveal itself. And yet, I know that this is easier said than done. For the addiction to fear and your adversity to the unknown will hold you back as it did for me.

I spent my entire life in denial of my calling. Choosing to derail every effort to seek out its Truth. Yet, as I look back on my life, I cannot do so without feeling a tremendous sense of gratitude and appreciation for the road I have traveled. You see, I have come to understand that each moment was laid out precisely the way it needed to be in order to experience it the way I did. Though there were moments I would never wish on anyone, I know that to have changed any aspect of one, even slightly, would have caused me to have missed this precise moment in my life.

"So where exactly is that?" you might ask. As I write this final chapter, I find myself in unfamiliar territory. Standing outside of my prison walls, or as Plato would have it, outside of the cave I call my mind. For the first time in my life, I can say with great humility, that I am free of my addiction to fear. That I have stepped into the unknown only to find that the world that was waiting for me was far more compassionate than the one I had inherited long ago.

Like Buddha, I have found enlightenment only to discover that enlightenment is never ending. Similarly, I have found that I too am never ending. Therefore, the reality I exist within is now filled with infinite possibilities. The world that seems to be unfolding in front of me is both absolute and illusory. It is as though I have entered a new dimension of consciousness created from both worlds. Created by everything that we as humanity have done in our efforts to experience ourselves as God through duality. An entirely new playground whereby I am free to dance with duality in my never ending quest to create a world based on my desire for peace, love, happiness and spiritual freedom. The core principles of our beingness.

Though this may sound rather esoteric, I assure it is not. For everything that I have been shown through Caleb tells me that the world that awaits is completely aligned with these principles. In fact, if I look closely enough, I can see yet another world that exists just beyond the sheath of this new reality. This is the world of my metaphysical existence. In time, this sheath will fade away giving rise to the reunion of all worlds. For now, I am free to jump in and out of each as I please. Using the power of my imagination to create portals to places that were once inaccessible other than through what we know of as death.

I have only begun to explore this incredible new world, but what I can tell you is that its energy is that of the Inner Child. A light so warm that it breathes life into every cell of my beingness. It is truly Heaven on Earth, but it is only now being born in a universe that has yet to be created. Know that this is not meant to be a metaphor. For this is simply the evolutionary process that we as God have known since the beginning. A process by which we will continue to experience ourselves forever.

In hindsight, I guess writing this book was my calling, or at least part of it. To capture in words this amazing process of discovery called the Awakening. To share it from the perspective of one man's quest to discover the Truth of who he really is. Along the way, discovering so much more than he had bargained for. So profound was the experience that he would be compelled to go back into his illusory cave to tell his fellow prisoners what he had seen. Only to find that most were unwilling, or better yet, unable to let go of their old ways.

I promised Caleb that I would let them have the last word, so I will leave you with these parting words of advice. To begin with, know that you are not alone. Know that you are part of a collective consciousness that has existed since way before time itself. Therefore, know that each and every one of you is "greatness" waiting to shine your light on humanity. Know that there could not be a more magnificent time to be alive. For what you are about to experience in this lifetime is everything that was promised to humanity long ago. Its beauty and grandeur will be unlike anything you have ever witnessed or dreamt of before.

No matter where you might be relative to your quest, remember to give your desires a fertile place to grow. In other words, do your best to never doubt your desires. Be faithful to them and they will shine. Know that conformity will always pull you away from who you truly are as a unique expression of God. Make it your goal to seek out your calling from this day forward regardless of what others may think or say of you. Remember, you came here to do something great and the time is NOW to do it!

Know that what you see as your physical reality is simply a reflection of you. There are no exceptions to this Universal Law. Therefore, it is absolutely imperative that you become that which you want to see in your world. Know that the inner quest is the key by which you will find the answers you are seeking. Let no one tell you differently – NO ONE! It is there, deep within the silence, that all will reveal itself. This too is a Universal Law.

Know that you must come to trust your inner Voice. Do not be afraid to let it guide you back to the light of your Inner Child. For your inner Voice represents the collective consciousness of what you have come to know as God which you, as the higher Self, are a part of. Know that the greatest feat you will ever accomplish is to take little to no physical action at all. But rather to focus, focus, focus your faith on what you desire to achieve. That is not to say that you will not take any action at all. But rather, the will to do so will come to you once the seeds of consciousness have taken hold within the roots of your desires.

Lastly, enjoy each and every moment of both your inner quest and outer journey. In time, you will come to appreciate how important they have been in defining your contribution to the Awakening. Nevertheless, it is time now for you to focus inwardly. For I assure you that if you do so, you will come to remember your calling.

There is so much more I want to share, but it will have to wait for another day or another book. The latter, being yet another aspect of my calling. Until then, I know our paths will cross again. It is simply unavoidable. For the magical, mystery ride we are about to embark on could never be as fascinating nor as fun without the two of us here to create it.

> *"Caleb, what is it that you would like to impart on humanity?" I asked, somewhat saddened that this would be their last contribution to this book. "Dear child, do not be saddened, for it is now time for humanity to write its own story." Caleb paused, as I could sense that each aspect of its consciousness was gathering itself for one last hurrah. "It is time for each of you to write your own story," Caleb continued. "And what a story it will be!*

"The discoveries you will make as you find your path back to the light will be nothing less than extraordinary. Know that the light of your Inner Child is waiting to come through and when it does, you will know the greatness that you are. As such, be not afraid for one day your light will shine brightly upon this world.

"Some of you have suffered mightily, having lost your alignment with the light long ago. What you have seen within the darkness of your fears we wish on no one. And yet, here you stand at the precipice of a new beginning. Having allowed yourself to willingly be guided by your inner Voice. A calling from somewhere deep within urging you to keep moving forward.

"For some, it may take time to fully embrace your call to greatness. Given the circumstances within which some of you have existed, that is to be expected. In fact, some of you will lose count as to how many times your inner Voice will be asked to intervene in talking you off the proverbial ledge. Know that this too is to be expected, for it is all part of your inner quest for the Truth.

"At some point, however, the knowledge and wisdom obtained from all of these encounters must be applied inwardly in some experiential manner. For you will never awaken to who you are and why you came here without these inward experiences. Therefore, we ask that you seek out your calling in whatever manner you are being shown to do so. Do not be afraid, for there are no right or wrong ways to this process.

"Know that what we have given you through this book was simply an outline to help you write your own story. Nevertheless, it is an outline full of so much knowledge and profound wisdom that we urge you to reference this book as often as you can. For your analytical mind will easily dismiss the messages hidden within its text. Discarding the words themselves as commonsensical. Never realizing how close you came to unlocking the nature of your true identity.

"In that vein, we have shown you the world of the original dream state. Knowing that few of you have been introduced to this state of beingness, much less understanding that you are still under its spell. The same applies to your knowledge of the inner world and the quest you will soon be asked to embark on. We have shown you how easy it is to captivate your mind relative to the exploits of your outer reality. Keeping your attention locked on the illusions of your physical world.

"Along the way, we introduced you to your inner Voice and its importance in helping you to cross the shifting waters of your inner voyage. Introducing you to the analytical mind and the world of the Left Brain Consciousness that controls every aspect of your physical reality. Hoping that you would soon come to realize that a world of consciousness was waiting for you deep within the serenity of your inner silence.

"Worlds known as the Right Brain Consciousness and the heart or God Consciousness. Worlds that

represent who you really are as non-physical. None of these worlds can be accessed by the physical body nor the analytical mind no matter how hard you try. And yet, try you will as if somehow your analytical mind knows better than the higher Self. Hence, our reasoning in showing you the trappings of the egoic mind in case you insist on going forward in this manner.

"To ensure that you are well equipped for your inner quest, we introduced you to the Attributes and showed you how to gain inner wisdom and knowledge that would be essential in understanding the coding mechanisms of the Game. A Game that was designed to manifest what you deemed to be real in the dualistic world of the dream state. Here again, we warned you that the egoic mind would discard these as meaningless in a world bent on rewarding you on action rather than inaction.

"We have alluded to how your mathematics, quantum sciences and other disciplines are now being used to understand the inner workings of the Game you know as your physical universe. We explained how all aspects of your outer reality are inter-connected by a network of neurons hardwired to you as Consciousness. Everything from the neurons in your body to those found in the darkest regions of space are part of this network. A network that cannot exist without the transmission of energy signatures you have come to know as feelings. Making the universe sensitive to your every thought and emotion.

"Universal Laws of Manifestation, such as the Probability of One and the Law of Resonance, were explained to help you understand that the power you hold in creating your reality is a function of where you place your attention at any moment in time. That nothing in the present moment of the Now is contingent on anything that preceded it. That within each moment lies a billion opportunities to create a new, physical reality. And that what causes this to happen lies in the resonate frequencies of what you desire.

"But as relevant as this may be, everything that you were shown was to prepare you for the Awakening. A spiritual Ascension into the higher states of consciousness that will be supported by a group of enlightened beings known as the Children. Many have come to know of the Children, but few of you suspected that you might be one of them. Much less, what that Truth might entail relative to your specific purpose here on earth.

"We shared with you a glimpse of how the Awakening would occur and for what purpose. Showing you how, over the next decade, the landscape of your earthly paradigms would begin to go through massive changes. Even as we speak, the physical landscape of Gaia is changing to accommodate the multitude of energy vortices that have sprung up all over your planet. The second Awakening has started and things have gotten very interesting to say the least!

"Know that the metaphysical world of your inner reality is also experiencing seismic changes. Changes that cannot be seen, but rather felt through your non-physical senses. Senses that are coming back online that will allow you to experience both your inner and outer realities in ways you could never have dreamt of before. Know again, this isn't something that is going to happen in the next decade or two. For this is happening throughout the universe right now!

"So you see, everything has been laid out for you in a way that should be simple to understand. And yet, that simplicity will likely be the reason why most of what you read will be discarded. The reason why this book will be read once and never looked at again. Here again, never realizing how close you came to uncovering the secrets behind your true identity and your purpose for being here.

"Do not take for granted what you have learned to remember. Nor should you assume that simply knowing what has been shared is enough. You must 'be' that which you have come here to remember. Then and only then will you be able to let go of your dependency of what you perceive to be Truth in your physical reality. Then and only then will you come to unlearn what the analytical mind has taught you to believe. Be the stillness and know that you are the I Am before anything ever was!

"It is the ego construct that will have you believe that you have learned everything you came here to remember in this school of life. That you are ready

to graduate or to help others in their Ascension process. Beware, for the ego construct only knows duality. Therefore, to know that you are awake but still identify yourself with the rational mind and the physical body, is to be asleep in the new dream state.

"Know that you are not the victim in your play of life. That this is simply a clever illusion supported by the egoic mind. You are and will always be the creator of your reality. This is a Universal Law that has no exceptions. And though we support you when you stand up and recognize that the emperor has no clothes, it is equally important that you realize that the emperor you speak of is you. It is you that stands naked to the Truth and yet refuses to acknowledge it!

"By now, many of you are seeing signs, clues and messages everywhere. There is simply no way to avoid them. The light of the Inner Child will make it almost impossible for you not to see them. Because of the energy you possess, you will soon resonate with this beautiful light in ways you have never done so before. Seeing or experiencing life in ways you may have taken for granted, but that now hold a profound meaning in your heart.

"In the world to come, you will use duality as a wizard would use a wand. Learning to use your abilities to create realities in an awakened state that has never been seen before. Knowing your relationship with one another so as to never fall asleep again. That is why the Awakening is required. For it is meant to lead

humanity away from duality and into the light of the Ascension process.

"Your lessons are complete and soon it will be time for humanity to graduate. To rejoice in the Oneness that you are nothing and yet everything to all. To awaken to a state of consciousness that was once accessible only to the greatest teachers of your time. Teachers such as Buddha, Krishna, Jesus, Babaji, Muhammad, Abraham, Job, Laozi, Confucius, Mary Magdalene, and so many others – male and female – whose names have been forgotten, but whose teachings live on among the indigenous people of your planet.

"What greater cause could there ever be but to assist humanity as it bears witness to the light of a new dawning? What greater calling could you have but to share the light of your Inner Child as humanity goes through this incredible transformation? Before you answer, we ask that you take a moment to pray, meditate and reflect upon what you have just read. Let it resonate throughout your beingness to the furthest depths of your soul.

"This is not a calling to be taken lightly, for you will be challenged every step of the way by your analytical mind and your fear of the unknown. Know that this calling is much greater than you or any other individual. It is born from the Source where all light, YOUR light, resonates to and from. As such, you can never run from it. For it is, and always will be, that which your soul desires.

"The time has come for YOU to be that light. To hold your brilliance as you shine upon the darkness of your world. To use that energy to call upon the universal light of the Inner Child that stands ready to usher in the greatest Awakening humanity has ever known.

"Blessed are they who have mastered the stillness from within, for they will come to know their Truth. That they are here to usher in humanity's Awakening, and will forever be known as the 'Children of the Light.' The light that shines brightly within us all!

"And with that said, our transmission with you is now complete!"

About The Author

Franco Romero is a bestselling author and spiritual teacher living with Sharlene, his wife of 25 years, his children Logan, Savannah and Sophia, and their dog Willie in St. Louis Park, Minnesota. As an infant, Franco had a near death experience that would lead to a series of clairvoyant encounters throughout his life. Abilities he was unwilling to recognize until an Awakening in his mid-40s. A spiritual event that would change his life forever. In addition to being a teacher, Franco holds two masters' degrees from the University of Minnesota and is co-founder of MyNurish, a formulator of superfood nutrition for the body, mind and soul.

CPSIA information can be obtained
at www.ICGtesting.com
Printed in the USA
BVHW042007120423
662235BV00013B/522